NK

By

Douglas Farrago

CHAPTER ONE

"Yo, look at this mother f&cker?", said the boxer on the double-end bag to the other boxer on the speed bag. That boxer, an angry light-heavyweight name Lionel, turned and stopped his rhythmic noise making exercise to stare at one of the weirdest sights he had even seen at Carlo's Gym. Staring back at them was a little man, a dwarf, dripping wet from being out in the rain way too long. His head was bald and glistened from the rain that had recently landed on it. There were abrasions both on his scalp and chin, not from an altercation, but from a poor job of shaving. Pretty soon all the noises at the gym stopped and everyone was staring.

People of different walks of life come into boxing gyms all the time. Some are fighters who want to train. Some are pretenders who want to prove how tough they are. Some are fans who just want to watch what is going on. The rest are made up of entourages, trainers, ex-fighters, managers, criminals, gamblers and degenerates. This was the norm for Carlo's Gym as well. Interestingly enough, boxing gyms also get their fair share of homeless people who have to be physically removed most of the time. It may not be politically correct, but people in the boxing business don't care what others think of them. All they know is that their facility cannot be a hangout for vagrants. Many get physically threatened and hurt before being thrown out. It's not fair but that's how it works in these gyms. This makes it even weirder that a disheveled dwarf, with no means to defend himself, would come inside.

"Hey, yo, it's a bug. Someone call the exterminator", said the fighter who first saw the dwarf. The other boxers laughed.

"I'm the exterminator", called out a boxer from the back whose real nickname was, in fact, Willie "The Exterminator" Robinson. "Let me squish this little shit", he said walking towards the dwarf.

And that is how Bug got his "new" name. It wasn't his real name, but he never really used his real name much in life anymore. He had been a nomad doing whatever it took to survive and took whatever name was given to him at the time. He worked at carnivals and was called Munchkin. He worked as a clown and was called Leprechaun. He worked as a professional wrestler for a sleazy promoter and was called Mini-Me, and on and on it went. He was now in his late fifties and had run out of options and money and hope. He was beyond depressed and tried killing himself multiple times but never could complete the act. On this day, and during this torrential rainstorm, he decided to just walk. Maybe he would get hit by a car because it's tough for a car to see a little person. He didn't care. Maybe he would be swept away in one of the bayous that were starting to overflow from the massive rain. It didn't matter. He had no plan but something was pulling him to that gym.

It was the light and sounds that first grabbed Bug's attention and directed him over to the Carlo's. He had been in Houston only for a few hours, hitchhiking from Louisiana. New Orleans was a good place to make money for dwarfs because he was an anomaly even on Bourbon Street. The problem was that as money came in to his pocket it also went out in the form of booze, women and the bets he owed. It was also a great place to get involved with the wrong people. It took three days on I-10 to hitchhike to Houston but he really didn't have a goal in going there. He just needed to get out of New Orleans fast and he just felt something inside telling him to move in that direction. It is easier for a little person to get picked up while hitchhiking because people think they are kids. Many drivers are genuinely concerned for what they think is a child on the road with his thumb out. Most are disappointed when they realize it is just a dwarf but usually give a ride anyway. And it got Bug to Houston pretty swiftly.

His last driver dumped him out in the rain but was it was good enough for Bug. That's when he started walking and found his new destination. The worn-down sign for Carlo's Gym hung over the entrance. The place was a throwback to the old gyms, which really means no one kept it up and it was falling apart. The equipment and ring weren't bad, but the boxing posters on the walls were old, faded and peeling. But it was alive at dusk with cars, lights, the sounds of bags being hit and buzzers going off. It drew the him to it like a butterfly to a flame and that is how he ended up being the center of attention and stopping all activity.

They circled him like a wounded animal and yet he remained calm because, amazingly enough, Bug was used to these situations.

"Look at this little shit," said one fighter.

"Who opened the door and let the cricket in?" said another.

"Hey, bug, you got a name?" asked the first fighter.

"Yeah, it's….." (he was interrupted)

"Fuck you, it's Bug. Hey, Jip, you want me to throw this little motherfucker out the door? He looks like another homeless bitch trying to get some money and stink this place up", said another boxer.

"Let him be," said Limpy, a middle-aged Hispanic man who hobbled over as if he had cerebral palsy.

From the dimly lit corner office came a 73-year-old white man with a large white mustache and a paunch for a belly who walked slowly over to the spectacle and parted the group like Moses and the Red Sea. He had a worn-out brown vest filled with boxing paraphernalia in it, such things as gauze and Vaseline. His glasses hung on the tip of his nose as if they were perpetually going to fall off but they never did.

"We don't take in people off the street. Please leave", Jip said.

"I am not from the street", replied the dwarf.

"You're wet and dirty and smell. We have work to do here. Get out."

"I may a little out of sorts but I just came in from out of town to dry off. Can I just stay until it stops raining?"

"Why are you here?" asked Jip, "There are plenty of places where you can dry off."

"I think I am supposed to be here", said Bug.

"Why?"

"I don't know".

"Not good enough, get...." At that moment an awkward young black man in his early twenties, with a t-shirt with a picture of Bambi on it, wandered over to look at him. He patted Bug on his head, took out a small towel and wiped his bald head dry. He smiled. Bug smiled back. "You're funny", said the man-child. "You are my new friend" and he grabbed Bug by the hand to show him around the gym.

"Oh, shit", said Jip aloud to himself as they walked off.

Limpy just looked at Jip and mouthed "What the fuck?" where upon Jip responded with, "Keep an eye out for this. This is weird."

"Will do."

CHAPTER TWO

Very few things bothered or interested the man-child. You really wouldn't know he was there at the gym unless you paid attention. He stayed in the background doing his chores and never stopped moving. At first glance he could be taken as extremely shy or extremely awkward. It didn't really matter because whomever interacted with him knew immediately that he was not normal. He was a very simple person with a lot of quirks, which made others think he was mentally disabled. But there was also a certain complexity and stoicism to him that was only recognizable if one paid attention.

Jip and his late wife took the boy in when he was five years old. They fostered him like so many other kids during that time, but the state never could find a home for him. He was also too much to handle for the special education program at the time. He was bullied by schoolmates and didn't learn things like others did. He saw things differently and acted differently. The school felt he needed to be moved to a facility just for children like himself. Jip and his wife would have none of that, so they officially adopted him. He was later diagnosed with severe autism and as time went on, his shyness worsened, and he became almost non-communicative. He could talk but rarely chose to do so. He was home schooled by Jip's wife who found he was not stupid but was limited due to how he learned. She got him through a high school level education, but this all stopped when she died from breast cancer when he was 18 years old.

Carlo's gym was an old ratty place that was connected to Jip's house. Jip was not Carlo. No one knew who Carlo was other than he was some Italian trainer who started the gym over fifty years earlier. The name stuck and was never changed because it was iconic. When Jip took it over there was not much left to the place and it was barely treading water. Initially it came back to life again for a short time but those days were gone as well. It was Jip who built the extension and their house right next to the gym with a small entryway connecting the two. Jip was a carpenter who made a living doing jobs here and there. He was known for his fine craftsmanship; something he transferred into his hobby of making clocks, which adorned the house he and his wife lived in.

Taking in the boy changed their world. He and his wife could not have kids and so this was a big undertaking. It was mostly his wife's idea, if not demand, but Jip grew to love the child even though the burden was high. That burden increased immensely when Jip's wife died. The child, through necessity, was able to learn to do the normal activities of daily living that we all are accustomed to; cleaning, washing, bathing, doing dishes, etc. In fact, the boy had an obsessive focus quality to him so that once he got a basic skill down, he perfected it. This role was a tremendous benefit to Jip who needed the help. Along with Limpy, they were able to keep Carlo's Gym going…though barely.

Jip's wife never liked boxing but she knew Jip did and accepted it. Jip, himself, was a pretty good boxer in his day and early on as a trainer he had some luck with a string of very competitive fighters that he worked with. This is what initially brought back the popularity of Carlo's Gym. The boy, however, was never allowed in the gym due to his awkwardness and the quality of people loitering in the place. Even though Jip would chase out the worst of the worst it still wasn't a great place for a child and this bothered Jip's wife. So, the boy would have to stay away. This changed after her death as Jip had no choice but to bring him over to the gym section to watch him and to help Jip with the physical tasks he could no longer do.

At first the fighters didn't know what to make of the boy but as time went by, and he grew into a man-child, most treated him with a certain indifference. It was as if he was their mascot. Some, however, were still cruel to him behind Jip's back and even sometimes in front of it. The boy seemed to disregard anything derogatory said to him as if he never even heard of any of it. He had an amazing gift that allowed him to do that. Some of the fighters would curse at him, push him or tease him and he just ignored it. His stoic quality allowed him to ignore it all and do his chores like cleaning the gym and keeping things in order. This was a great benefit to Jip who needed all the help he could get. Unfortunately, it wasn't enough because there was so much to do managing the place. This included not only the physical tasks but also taking care of the fighters and doing the books. Jip knew that if he ever got sick then there would a major problem for not only the boy, who would have to be put in a home, but for the gym as well.

As the boy grew into a man-child, Jip started taking him with him to the morning runs that the boxers did. Soon the boy was running with them. It was great exercise for him, like treadmill therapy for an anxious dog, and he really was a natural. Over time he got into great shape. It was then that Jip realized that his adopted son had exceptional physical abilities and even excelled in some things that no one would expect.

As time went on, the boy became even more introverted and never really talked to anyone except Jip. Rarely, he would say a few words to Limpy but that was about all. With the fighters he would either smile or stare right through them, but never would interact with anyone outside of his closed-knit group.....until now.

CHAPTER THREE

"Look at that, a midget and a retard", said one of the fighters as the boy led Bug to another area. The next thing everyone heard was Jip slapping the fighter across the back of the head with an open hand, hard enough to almost drop him to his knees.

The boy's isolation always worried Jip but that was what kept his son comfortable and happy. This also contained the boy from having the rare anger outburst from occurring. They seemed to have stopped over the years. During a regular 24-hour period he was mostly in his own world doing his tasks while the fighters worked out. He hardly ever acknowledged them even when they pretended to engage him in a conversation, which was really a joke in disguise. He was now a young man and the only time he really would spend with his father was to watch boxing on television. But there was something different in the way he "knew" the dwarf, and this puzzled the old man. Jip thought maybe his son was using the dwarf as some sort of toy. He was confused because he never connected with anyone in the gym before, especially someone new.

The boy brought Bug to the room where the cleaning supplies were and pulled out a tattered spiral notebook and showed it to him. It was one of many he kept there. Bug saw pages and pages of notes on every fighter that has ever been through Carlo's Gym since the boy could remember. There were notes on each fighter's style, his conditioning, his weakness, what type of fighter would give him trouble, what he could do to be better, and on and on. Bug was amazed. The boy didn't seem like he had the capacity to author such a thing. The penmanship was meticulous. There were pictures and notations. It was a brilliant manual. Bug wondered why he was showing this to him.

The boy put out his hand and said, "Noki".

"Sam….er..well, I guess you can call me Bug"

"I like you, Bug".

"Um, I guess I like you too, Noki."

When they left the janitor's closet, Jip called Bug over to him and Noki went over to clean some of the water buckets from the ring.

"What's your story, little man?" asked Jip

"I have a long story, but it really doesn't mean anything to anyone. I'm a wanderer but I mean no harm to you or your son. That's your son, right? "

"Yes, Noki is my son. He's black, I'm white. So what?"

"I'm not judging…"

"I adopted him and he and this gym is all I have".

"We'll, he's special…."

"He's not retarded. And he is very special to me. He is just autistic and very tough to reach. For some reason he has taken to you. That has never happened before. Why is that?"

"I don't know."

"What did you do to him? What did he show you?"

"He just showed me around, really, that's all".

"This is weird." The old man paused for a minute. "Listen, I'm too old to figure anything out any more. We're closing soon so come back tomorrow and we'll see what happens".

"Okay."

"Why did you come here again, anyway?"

"I really don't know."

CHAPTER FOUR

Bug left the gym in the dark with nowhere to go. As he left, he felt different. He felt some sort of purpose in his life that he couldn't figure out. Slowly leaving the driveway he meandered right and then left and the started to walk to find some sort of shelter or place to sleep. He knew the routine because he had done it so many times before. Just sign in at the place and be respectful and you have a cot to sleep on. That was good enough for him. He just had to find a place. The rain had slowed to a drizzle. That's when he heard the old man again, trailing him in a car.

"You are homeless, aren't you?" Jip said from the rolled down window of the vehicle.

"For the moment, yes."

"Come back with me. But if you tell anyone you are homeless then I will throw your little ass out."

"Uh, okay…."

Jip lead Bug back to the same janitor's closet where Noki showed him the notebook. It was small but big enough for a little person. The bathroom was the community bathroom located in the locker room, at the other end of the gym. Jip pulled out a small cot and unfolded it for him.

"You can stay the night. Maybe you can serve a purpose for me. I don't know. We'll talk. I need more help than Noki or Limpy can give me but maybe the biggest thing is you being able to communicate with Noki."

"Sounds great. Thank you".

"Don't thank me. Thank Noki. One mistake and you're gone. You hear me?"

"Yes, sir".

Bug was able to settle down in his cot. He was as confused as anyone. The sleeping conditions didn't bother him. He had been in infinitely worse conditions before. He also wondered if he was being used as a plaything for the man-child but he didn't care. The place was warm and dry. A knock on the door interrupted his thoughts as the old man gave him a plate from the dinner he had eaten earlier with Noki.

"Here, you're hungry."

"Thank you".

"You need clothes, but I have no idea how to fit you into anything. I'll find some of Noki's old stuff as a child. We save everything so maybe they'll fit. I'll also take you to Goodwill tomorrow."

"You are more than kind."

"Yeah, well don't tell anyone. I don't need that reputation with some of the son-of-a-bitches that run around this place. Getting them to pay their dues is hard enough. I don't need anyone seeing me giving handouts."

"You got it".

"One mistake and…"

"I know…and I'm out of here".

CHAPTER FIVE

The sound from the gym woke Bug up. It was still dark outside, so he thought maybe the gym was being robbed. One of the few possessions Bug had was a wind-up pocket watch from his carnival days. It said 10:02. The rattling was bone shattering and Bug was scared. He clicked his bedside lamp on and looked around the closet and found a mop handle. Slowly he opened the door to see what was making the racket. Petrified, he held the mop handle as if it was a baseball bat and slowly walked into the gym area. He froze in his last step when he saw it. There on the heavy bag was Noki, now wearing a t-shirt with Mowgli from the Jungle Book on the front, putting on an exhibition of his boxing technique. It was poetry as he worked the bag. There was no timer but Noki just seemed to know when a three-minute round was up. Bug just stared in disbelief. Noki knew he was there but didn't seem to care. There was a certain trust he had given Bug. The dwarf slowly walked out and Noki stopped just for a second to look at him and smile and then he went back to work. After three rounds he moved to the double-end bag and then the speed bag. Bug was hypnotized by it all. He knew little of boxing, other than being a fringe fan of some of the most famous fighters he had seen on TV over the years, but he was aware how good this kid was.

For the last three rounds Noki shadowed boxed and moved around inside the elevated ring. He was a maestro, a masterful dancer. His moves were as fluid as an artist. For the first round, he looked at

Bug and said, "Ali" and began mimicking every move that "The Greatest" used. Bug smiled. Then Bug got him some water before he began the second round whereupon Noki said, "Alexis Arguello" and began the hand position and movement of one of the greatest Nicaraguan fighters ever. For the last round he said "Frazier" and he became the replica of Smoking Joe. Even his posture changed as he bobbed his head as if he was fighting Ali. The boy transformed himself into each fighter as if he was that person. This was a show that Bug thoroughly enjoyed and thought everyone else would as well. But he instinctively knew he was the only one ever to see it.

"You are amazing", Bug told the boy when he was done. Noki just smiled. When he was done, he took some water from bottle Bug got for him and then toweled himself off.

"But how do you know how to do this?"

"I like boxing". Noki then grabbed him by the wrist and walked him through the connector into Jip's house. They slowly walked by Jip's room who was sleeping with his cat and a bowl with a large goldfish next to his bed. The sound of the clocks on the walls and the snoring by Jip was so loud that there was no way the old man would wake up.

After walking upstairs, and upon entering Noki's room, Bug became overwhelmed with what he saw. There were pictures and posters of great fighters all over the room. There were more binders like the ones he had shown him from the janitor's closet. What was more interesting was the hundreds and hundreds of VHS tapes lined up in perfect alphabetical order filling all the empty spaces in the boy's room. Noki took one of the tapes and put it in the player and had Bug sit down. For the next hour they watched the fights of Billy Conn and Jack Dempsey. Bug had heard of these fighters before but never seen them fight. As they watched he was able to see the immense focus in Noki's eyes. He never smiled and seemed to never blink. The only time he would look away was to write something in his notebook.

After an hour or so Noki shook Bug's hand, which obviously meant goodnight. Bug seemed to immediately understand and walked out of Noki's room. He heard the shower go on as he went downstairs and traveled past Jip's room once again. It was midnight and the wall clocks were all chiming and making their own special noises. This and Jip's snoring made his footsteps silent as he walked towards the connector and back into the gym. As he made his way to his janitor's closet, he stared at the ring almost reliving what he had seen earlier with Noki dancing like around. He smiled, shook his head, shut the gym lights off, and picked the mop handle up from the floor. Shutting the door behind him, he laid on his cot and listened to the raindrops hit the metal roof of the gym. He checked his pocket watch which said 12:13 and then clicked off of the lamp next to his bed and fell immediately asleep. His first good sleep in a very long time.

CHAPTER SIX

The knock at his door made Bug fall immediately off the cot. Bug didn't even know where he was. It was six in the morning and the sun was just coming up.

"Get up and help me with the morning workouts", screamed Jip.

"Morning workouts?" Bug loudly asked back from behind the door.

"Just get dressed and get out here. I am leaving some of Noki's old clothes outside of the door. You have five minutes."

Bug opened the door and found some shorts and a shirt with a picture of Cinderella on the front. Bug was uncomfortable putting it on but did so anyway. He put on his shoes and raced out the door. Waiting for him in the car was Noki and Jip. Noki was actually the one to drive them to the local park where there was a three-mile running loop. Three fighters were already there and another showed up a minute later.

"Okay, Lionel has got a major fight in three months. He needs this win because he'll get a shot at the championship. Let's be somewhat of a team here. Stay together but keep up Noki's pace. "

"Ok, Noki, have them run seven and a half minute miles".

Noki just smiled. Noki was wearing another Disney shirt, this time with the dragon from Sleeping Beauty.

Lionel didn't even acknowledge Jip or Noki. He just started his run while others were stretching. It was an alpha move to show who the most important person was. Noki caught up to him pretty quickly and off they went.

"Why am I here?" asked Bug

"Well, I want you to see what we do. I also want to talk".

"About Noki?"

"Yes. I told you he is all I got. He may seem wooden and lifeless to others, but there is so much more to him. He is pure goodness. Sure, he has got his quirks and stuff, but he is a great kid."

"I like him."

"Good. And for some reason he has taken a liking to you. Not sure why but let's see how this plays out. Maybe he'll get tired of you but if this sticks then you can stay around."

"Really? You're serious?"

"Yes".

"I can't thank you enough."

"Don't get too used to it because I have a low tolerance for bullshit and have been burned before".

"You have my word. I have nowhere else to go so no bullshit."

"That means no drinking and no smoking."

"Oh. Ok, I understand and thank you." There was a minute or so pause when Bug spoke up again. "You know, Noki really loves boxing."

"I know. He's obsessed with it but at least it's a healthy obsession."

"And he looks like he could be a great fighter himself".

"How would you know?"

"Well, I saw him work out last night."

"What? Shit, I thought he stopped that. Dammit. He must wait until after I'm asleep. What did you see?"

"I saw him hit the bags and then shadow box."

"It's amazing, isn't it?"

"Yes, it is. Has he ever had an organized match anyone?"

"No. First my wife would not let it happen and then I could not let it happen"

"Why not?"

"Because he is so special to me. I would never want him to get hurt. I know I am a boxing trainer but it's different with your own family. No one wants to see their child get hurt but at least with a normal kid you know it is his choice. With Noki, who knows? I don't know if he understands the concept that someone wants to hurt him? Does he know that his own life is on the line? I have wrestled with that for a long time. It's like dog fighting where they put some untrained, weak dog in there to be slaughtered by the pit bull. Your heart sinks."

"You don't think he could handle himself for real?"

"You don't think I didn't prepare him for life. The ONLY thing I could teach him was boxing and so I did. To defend himself. I did it when my wife wasn't looking. I would tutor him but it was what he learned more by watching others in the gym and on TV. The weird thing is he sees things differently than we do. Sure, he can't pick up emotional things because of his autism. He is socially awkward. An odd duck. But he can look at pictures and films in a way that we can't and then his brain makes it work for him in a physical manner."

"Like some type of idiot savant?"

"He isn't an idiot but yes, he is a savant about a few things and one of them is boxing. He can mimic any fighter he wants. He can also break down the tape of any fighter he sees and decipher tendencies others cannot understand."

"So, I guess you must have let him box before? Did it not go well?"

"Yeah, not go well (Jip laughs). That's what we had to say to the sparring partners as we picked them up off the canvas."

Bug's eyes opened liked saucers. There was a pause and then Bug asked, "You said he is a savant about a couple of things. What else?"

"Well, when he was young kid, and even teenager, we let him watch cartoons. Mostly Walt Disney movies on VHS. He was obsessed. Maybe too obsessed. It was before his interest in boxing. He would watch the movies over and over again. We couldn't get him to stop and do other things. It's part of his quirkiness".

"That's why he has all the shirts?"

"Yup. He wears them out and I have to find new ones. He used to wear one all the time. It got gross. Anyway, the wife and I got a chance to take him to Walt Disney World once. He loved it. I have to say it was one of our greatest experiences together. He studied it before we went and knew everything about the place. He was our tour guide without ever even going before. That's what Noki does. It was costly, though. I also wanted to go again so I tried to save up for it but then my wife got ill".

Before Bug could ask any more about it, Jip had him get out of the car to walk over to where the fighters were finishing their run.

Noki was well ahead of any fighter in the run and when he finished, he led them to an area of the park where they stretched some and then they all went their separate ways. Lionel was the closest to finishing after Noki. He didn't stretch but instead went right to the car where John, a trainer, was sitting in the driver's seat and left. He never said goodbye.

Noki, Jip and Bug went to breakfast at a local diner. These were normally very quiet meals. Noki, usually didn't talk much but instead would stare at his food while he ate. With Jip, he may give yes and no answers. Today was just a little different. Bug would ask Noki more open-ended question and if it pertained to something Noki liked, i.e. boxing, then Noki would say full sentences. And he even started to turn to look at Bug in the eyes when he answered. This did not go unnoticed by Jip.

As they walked to the car Jip whispered to Bug, "You can stay a little longer".

Bug just smiled.

CHAPTER SEVEN

The days and nights were almost exactly the same as time went on. Boxing training is a repetitive sport with very few changes. It's not very exciting and the regimen is monotonous where the same things happen over and over again. The only difference now at Carlo's Gym was that Bug was getting a little more responsibility from Jip. After a few weeks he even learned a few of the behind-the-scenes financials that Jip was dealing with, which, he found out, weren't that good. Getting boxers to pay their monthly fees was extremely hard. They always had an excuse why they didn't have the money. Some were legit but many were just lying. Jip found it hard to keep track of these things so Bug started reminding him as the boxers walked through the door.

"Owes money", he pointed to one boxer. "Paid up", he pointed to another. "New and never paid", he said once more.

This was just a way to remind Jip to give them one last warning and then stop and turn them away if this was ignored. In return for his help Bug was allowed to stay in the gym and was even given a nominal stipend.

"Boxing is a crooked game", Jip would tell Bug, "Everyone involved is a liar".

Bug felt right at home. It was just another profession of criminals he had to deal with. He had done it before and was unfazed by it all.

"They will all screw you over, one time or another. Do not trust anyone", Jip continued.

"Then why do you trust me?" Bug asked.

"Because Noki does. No other reason. Besides, who else can I trust? Maybe Limpy, a little, but he really doesn't have the capacity to help much. I saved him years ago like I saved you. I don't think he would screw me, but he can't do much to help me especially with Noki."

"How about John?"

"John? This sounds bad but I wouldn't trust him as far as I could throw him. "

John Maxwell was in his early 60s. He had been around the game his whole life. He turned to training fighters in his thirties and has a pretty good reputation locally but nothing on a national or world championship level. He was a constant at the gym, though, and started helping out Jip now and then both for training and as a cutman. Cutmen are not doctors. They need no training other than what they get on the job and with experience working with other cutmen. Through a non-official apprenticeship, and having the right equipment and medications, they create their reputation in the boxing world. John was a pretty good cutman and for $50 you can rent him for your fight. But John was a fixture at Carlo's Gym in order to find his own big break and Jip knew it. Still, he served a purpose in helping fighters, especially Jip's prized pupil, Lionel.

"Well, you can trust me," said Bug.

"We'll see", Jip replied.

Each day was like the next. Every morning, except Sundays, Bug would go to the park where the boxers met for a run and every late afternoon he would help out at the gym when fighters would spar and train. At 10:02 PM he would hear Noki come in and go out to hang out with him. Noki would change up which fighter he would imitate, and they would end the night late by watching old boxing films. It became soothing for Bug. It didn't bore him. It actually gave him some comfort. It was therapy. He enjoyed the security of a routine and he was constantly enamored and amazed by Noki. His focus, and intensity, were palpable. Noki's memory, about boxing, was photographic. Soon Noki's conversations included longer sentences, but only with Bug. And every night Jip would snore through it all.

CHAPTER EIGHT

"I'll knock any mother fucker out in this place!".

The man was large. Very large. He just walked in the gym from off the street and started screaming that same sentence over and over again to anyone who would listen..

"I'll knock any mother fucker out in this place!"

The boxers in the gym that afternoon initially went silent with the screaming coming from the combative newbie but instantly went back to hitting their bags or shadowboxing. It was as if they had seen this guy before, but they hadn't. They had just seen this scenario happen over and over again throughout the years. It's a bizarre ritual. Some idiot, without boxing skills thinks he is King Kong and wants to show how tough he is. They "write checks their ass can't cash", as Limpy told Bug.

"Hey, old man! Put me in with your best!"

"Can you box?" asked Jip

"I'm the baddest motherfucker there is. Give me your best!"

"Noki…..glove up".

Bug had been there for a month and never saw Noki actually box with anyone. He just saw him do his thing at night. There was laughter by the boxers in the gym as they saw Noki get sparring gear on. Bug feared they were mocking Noki but they weren't.

"There are still rules in boxing. No hitting behind the head or below the belt. No wrestling. Protect yourself at all times", John told both Noki and the street bully.

"Get ready to get hurt", screamed the street bully at Noki. Noki just stared. "Did you hear me mother fucker? Say goodnight." Noki just kept staring. Jip went over to Noki and said "Floyd Mayweather Jr. Just tend to business."

Floyd Mayweather was regarded as one of the best fighters of all time. His foot movement and defense were impeccable, and he just seemed to never get hit. He won championships in five different weight classes and was a master of the ring.

For two and a half minutes of the three-minute round Noki danced around the ring as the bully swung and missed wildly. At first it was with a lot of force, but by the end of the round the bully could hardly move his arms. Noki did his best imitation of Floyd, moving around like a matador and barely breaking a sweat. He did not throw a single punch. With about 15 seconds left in the round Jip told Noki "Okay" and Noki threw a 12-punch barrage to the body of the bully, which made him wince and squeak like a wounded pig. When the bell rang the bully ripped off his gloves and headgear and walked briskly out of the same door he had come in yelling fifteen minutes earlier and he was never to be heard from again.

The fighters all went back to their training. Noki got his gear off and went back to doing his chores. Jip went back to instructing some other boxers. It was bizarre because they acted like nothing had ever happened. Bug was stunned.

"Why don't you let him spar with others?" he asked Jip later in his office.

"I don't want to talk about it" Jip replied.

"You said he doesn't get beaten, right?"

"Correct."

"Does he not want to box?"

"That's all he ever asked me to do was to let him fight".

"So why not let him?"

"We tried once but things went bad."

"He got hurt?"

"No. I picked the wrong person for him to imitate."

"Who?"

"Just let it be. I'd rather not say."

"And what happened?"

"He almost killed the guy, okay. This was about three years ago. He doesn't understand things. He just does what you tell him and like a robot goes about it doing it. He promised me he would never fight like that again, but I still couldn't let him spar anymore. Not worth the risk."

"But you did today?"

"Yeah, for these idiots who come waltzing into the place trying to show everyone up I will allow it. I just tell him to fight like Mayweather, tend to business and then only hit to the body. "

"Is he okay with not sparring anymore?"

"No. I think he resents me for it. I can't tell. That's why he does his thing at night, I guess. At least I give him these moments".

"How often does some idiot come in here screaming?"

"About every other month".

"It sure seems to make him happy. How come you never give him another chance to spar with regular fighters?"

"Because I promised my wife. She was afraid they would take him away from us if he hurt anyone. She's right. So, stop asking."

"I'm not judging, and no disrespect to your wife, but if Noki really can fight and loves to do it then why not let him try?"

"Listen, little man, my wife and Noki are all I have...or had in this world. One is gone. I can't risk anything happening to the one I have left. Do you get that?"

"I do. I do. I'm sorry".

"Besides, I have more to think about. Gideon's fight is in less than two months and we are losing sparring partners left and right. If he wins this fight, he is guaranteed a shot at the championship. Do you know what that means?"

"That he'll be champion?"

"Figured that out all by yourself? Of course, he'll be champion, but it also means we can have a good source of money coming in here."

"Are things that bad?"

"I showed you some of the financials. These boxers only pay half the time to work out here. That's on a good month. We just get by. Lionel Gideon is our golden ticket. I manage and train him. Been doing it since he was 15 years old. I discovered him and got him out of a bad home situation. If he gets this belt then we are on easy street."

"I was on easy street once."

"And?"

"It wasn't that easy."

Chapter Nine

Limpy helped the injured fighter out of the ring. Lionel Gideon had done a number on him during his sparring session. Jip was not amused and knew there would be consequences. Bug went into the locker room and saw Limpy putting ice on the young kid's head. He was concussed, but okay, and his own trainer was trying to talk to him. Limpy gave the ice bag to the trainer and walked away.

"Not fun for these guys, huh?" Bug asked Limpy.

"They know what's going on," Limpy said in a husky voice. Limpy knew the deal. He, too, was a great prospect as an amateur. He was an up and coming Hispanic hero to his local friends and family and had a bright future. To make ends meet he would do manual labor and his career ended when he shattered both his lower legs in a freak accident. He went through tons of surgeries but was never the same. He lost it all. He could no longer fight competitively and now walked with a severe limp. His life spiraled out of control afterwards and though he made some money off the lawsuit from the accident, he went through it quickly partying and a bad lifestyle. He was in tough shape until he met up with Jip a year later. Jip was able to get him a job at a local health club for the rich and he actually did well there doing some training and cleaning equipment. It was enough to get him back on his feet and he repaid Jip by coming to Carlo's and helping out with some of the fighters. It also made him feel good to be close to the game. He just loved being around boxers and wanted to be a trainer like John and Jip. He was a good man but not the heir apparent that Jip needed to take over the place.

"This is not going to be good for us", Limpy told Bug.

"Why?"

"Ain't no more fighters to get to spar with Lionel".

"And that's bad?"

"Real bad. He needs to spar. He needs the rounds, homey."

"I'm sure Jip will figure it out."

"He can't just wish for fighters to show up. No one else here is going to work with him. They're afraid".

Jip was not himself when Bug saw him later. He was lost in thought and frantically making phone calls. Bug didn't want to bother him, so he helped clean up and then closed the gym down when the fighters left. Later that night he watched Noki do his thing on the bags and in the ring. While watching old fights on tape he asked Noki about Lionel.

"So, do you think Lionel will win the title soon?"

"Yes."

"What makes you so sure?"

Noki put in some tapes of Lionel's past fights. He was a stone, cold killer. The fights were short because he kept knocking guys out quickly. Bug's eyes were glued to the television. He knew why Jip needed Lionel because he was that good.

"Can anyone beat him?"

"Yes and no."

"What does that mean, Noki?"

"He's not perfect."

"Meaning?"

Noki brought out his notebook that he now kept in his room and showed it to Bug. There were pages of notes that went over everything that Lionel did. Noki noticed that was very strong and always stalked his prey. He never backed up and had good defense but since his fights were short, he really never was tested in the later rounds. His side-to-side motion was not great and his style was always the aggressor. No one hit him to the body, which may be a weakness for him. Noki also noted that no one pushed him backwards on to his heels to see how he could handle that.

"Did you share this with Jip?"

"No."

"How about Lionel?"

"No"

"You have a gift, Noki. You should share it."

"No. Just with you", Noki said with a little louder voice. He was upset.

"Okay, my friend, okay", replied Bug.

The two just watched some of Marvin Hagler's best fights until it was bedtime. In his cot Bug tried to figure out how Noki could share his knowledge with others but never found an answer. It saddened him that Noki was not treated by most as if he mattered or was a real person. He fell asleep with those thoughts and was awakened a few hours later for the morning run.

The gym was not the same for the next few weeks. Jip was noticeably bothered by something. Gideon, too, was in a caustic mood and made his emotions obvious to the journalists who would come to interview him because the fight was getting closer. The other issue is that he had no one to spar anymore. He just worked the hand pads with John.

As the last fighters left the gym you could hear Jip yelling through the closed door of his office. "What do you mean he won't spar? Damn it, the fight is only three weeks away. I need someone for Gideon. "

Lionel Gideon was an unhappy man. Not just these past few days but every day. Contrary to what people think, most fighters are actually nice people. There are a few famous ones who were portrayed as mean but truth be told, it's rare. But Lionel Gideon was one of them. He hated everyone. The better his record got the worse he treated people, especially Jip and......Noki.

It was not uncommon for Gideon to make fun of Noki and mock him on the morning runs or in the gym. When Noki offered him the spit bucket after Lionel Gideon took some water he would purposefully miss and make sure to hit Noki with some.

Of all the people he terrorized, he saved most of his contempt for Jip. No one knew why. Jip did everything for him. He discovered Gideon as a kid and taught him everything he knew. And it worked. Gideon climbed the light-heavyweight ranks by crushing his opponents. The better fighters went out of their way not to fight him, which made getting him a title shot very hard. He was now finally in a spot to get a mandatory title fight if he won this next match.

Jip sacrificed more and more for the kid and that was part of the gym's troubles. In order to make Gideon happy he allowed John to work with him full time, which put a strain on the gym's workforce. Limpy had to handle more duties and extend himself to organize and watch over the other fighters in the gym. He held hand pads for some of the fighters and also gave them instruction. Noki and Bug would do all the nasty work. They would clean the place and wash things. They would help out if anybody needed anything. They would get water for fighters and help them out in the corner during sparring. Jip became more of an overseer now. Due to his advancing age he also would spend most of his time in his office doing paperwork, making phone calls, and just looking stressed out. Bug continued his apprenticeship

37

with Jip learning the back end of how the gym works. When Gideon came in the gym to work out each day, Jip would come out there for him but John did all the heavy lifting. It was starting to get awkward as people wondered who really was training, and in charge, of Lionel Gideon: John or Jip?

CHAPTER TEN

The next afternoon Jip was pacing around the office. As fighters started to begin their workouts he came out and looked around.

"Noki, come here."

Noki hurried to his Dad.

"I need you to spar with Gideon today".

Noki just shook his head in agreement. There was no hesitation. It was like a little kid getting a surprise present or about to get on a roller coaster, except this roller coaster could get him killed. Noki took off to the house to get his mouthpiece.

"Why are you doing this?" Bug asked Jip as he overhead the conversation.

"I don't want to talk about it" Jip responded and walked back into his office. Bug followed him.

"What about that whole song and dance about promising your wife?"

"I have no choice anymore."

"But Noki can get hurt. I have seen Gideon fight."

"He won't."

"How do you know that?"

"Because he will do what I tell him to do."

"You mean Gideon will take it easy? He never takes it easy on anyone."

"No, Noki will".

"Is Noki good enough? Can he really fight?"

"Of course, he can fight. You've seen him practice at night. He's special. I taught him at first but the more he studied, the better he got."

"But Gideon is one of the best in the world."

"I know. Listen, I'm stuck. This place is full of rats. I could lose Gideon and then we lose this place. I have no choice."

"So, you sacrifice your son?"

"Listen, you little shit, I gave you a home and a job. Who are you to question me?"

"It's not about questioning you. I appreciate everything you gave me, but I have seen this kind of thing my whole life. The weak being exploited by the powerful. That was me. I don't know why I ended up here, but it seems that part of it is to protect Noki"

"Great. I want that. Protect him. I don't know how much longer I will be on this planet and I want someone to be there for him.

Maybe that is why I have given you so much responsibility. And he trusts you. You're basically his conscience. That being said, I fear bad people are going to take Gideon away unless I make him happy and get him some sparring".

"And if you don't?"

"Then he walks. And we go bankrupt. And then what happens to you? Or Noki? None of us will have a pot to piss in." With that Jip walked away to prepare for the sparring session. Noki was already putting his equipment on. Gideon was working some hand pads in the ring with John to get warmed up.

"You putting me in the ring with a retard? That's all you got for me, old man?"

Jip ignored him and whispered to Noki "Willie Pep... and remember just to tend to business".

Guglielmo Papaleo, better known as Willie Pep, held the World Featherweight championship twice between the years of 1942 and 1950. Pep boxed a total of 1,956 rounds in the 241 bouts during his 26-year career. He was known for his incredible footwork and knack for not getting hit. His ability to spin and create angles by moving his feet was uncanny and rumors have it that he actually won a round in a major fight without throwing a punch. Noki knew exactly what Jip wanted him to do. And Jip obviously knew some of same weaknesses about Gideon that Noki knew.

When the bell rang Gideon came out like he always does, pressing straightforward and throwing punches with mean intentions. Not only did he want to get a good workout in, but he wanted to teach Noki, and Jip, a lesson. Who was this little punk, with no fights under his belt, to even be in the same ring as him, a world contender?

Noki immediately went into Willie Pep mode. Gideon threw haymakers to hurt Noki but missed wildly. Noki spun and evaded everything and then gave a few punches to Gideon's body. This made Gideon even madder. Noki only threw a few punches to the Gideon's head while Gideon threw combination after combination. It turned about to be an exhausting round for the would-be champ, which should have met his goal and made him happy. He needed these types of training sessions. Instead, all the gym stopped to watch, which embarrassed Gideon and made him more pissed.

Bug helped Noki between rounds by washing his mouthpiece and getting Vaseline on him. It was his first time helping out between rounds with a fighter and he didn't know what to really say.

"Great job, Noki. Keep doing what you are doing. You aren't here to win. You just need to not get hit, okay?" Noki nodded. He was unfazed. There was no noticeable fear in his demeanor. This amazed Bug would who was doing everything in his power not to shit his own pants.

Jip came over and said, "Okay, Noki, you're doing great. I am proud of you. I don't need you to try and hit him. Bang the body, fine, but no major combinations. I don't want you hurt or him hurt". Noki nodded. He was loving this.

"Aren't you handicapping him?" Bug asked Jip.

"He's good enough to do what I said. We don't want a war here. We just need to get through this and get Gideon a workout."

The second round was about the same. But Gideon was not on the same page as Jip or Noki as he truly was trying to create damage with his punches. Bug's stomach turned with each knockout attempt by Gideon. He had never been so nervous in his life. Noki, on the other hand, was relaxed and having a great time. He was doing what he seemed to be born to do. He spun, danced and defended himself beautifully. That is when Gideon started talking during the action.

"C'mon, bitch. Stand here and fight".

Noki's expression never changed. He didn't acknowledge anything that Gideon said. It was as if he never heard it.

"Retards can't fight. Be a man and let's do this, bitch."

Noki slipped a massive hook and spun to throw a right hand that just missed Gideon's face. It was as if Noki held back, which he did. When the bell rang, and as Noki stopped fighting, Gideon threw a massive right hand that grazed the top of Noki's head. A last second head movement by Noki saved him from crashing to the ground.

"Hey, stop that shit", Bug yelled.

"Fuck you, midget. You're next!" yelled Gideon and all the color washed from Bug's face.

Jip told John to have Gideon keep it clean, knowing that his words to Gideon would mean nothing. They never did.

In the corner Bug told Noki to just keep moving. "Don't make him mad." It was a weird thing to say to Noki who was doing everything right. He had no comprehension of what egging someone on was. He showed no expression in the ring. He didn't taunt. He didn't showboat. He was just doing his job, and this is what pissed off Gideon even more.

The third, and last sparring round, was more of the same. It became obvious that Gideon was not enjoying himself like Noki was. The crowd watching even made it worse. This was embarrassing for Gideon and he was not going to have any more of it. Halfway through the round Gideon caught Noki in the corner by trapping Noki's right arm with his left arm. With intense pressure he squeezed that arm and twisted it so tight that Noki was in a compromised position. In sparring sessions there are no refs to stop an illegal move. The outside cornermen usually yell for the fighters to stop and break it up. It was too late for that. Gideon, with all his years of experience of being dirty, yanked on Noki's arm and began hitting him with his free right arm on top of and behind Noki's head. Noki was stunned. He didn't understand dirty fighting. This was not the art of boxing he studied. Gideon reigned punches and Noki was taking them and was starting to get hurt. Jip yelled but to no avail. John said nothing the whole time but instead stood there in Gideon's corner with a smirk on his face. Bug jumped in but was pushed to the ground by Gideon's free right arm. Jip, the old man, was able to climb into the ring and get in the middle. He even took a few punches himself. Gideon finally let go.

"Put a retard in the ring with me old man? This is what you get. I am the best in the world. Fuck you and fuck this place."

"Go get dressed!" Jip angrily responded.

"Fuck you, old man!" screamed Gideon as he left the ring and went to the locker room with John following in tow.

"Are you okay, Noki?" Jip asked.

Noki nodded yes. Bug looked at Jip and could see tears in his eyes. He saw how broken up and torn he was. He finally understood how Jip was truly was caught between a rock and a hard place. Things were not going to be the same.

CHAPTER ELEVEN

Jip stayed in his office for hours after the sparring debacle. Bug took to caring for Noki, who was luckily doing fine. The shades were drawn in Jip's office as he cried. He tried to keep himself busy with paperwork and bills. The gym was dark and empty now. Bug didn't want to bother Jip and he went about his chores cleaning up around the place. Noki did his jobs too and then went back into the house. At around 9 PM the phone rang.

"But you can't do that," Jip said, "We have a contract."

"You won't win a lawsuit," John responded from the other end of the phone, "You have no money, and no one will take the case. Gideon's not happy. He is going to the gym across town. He wants to move on. Thinks you can't take him to the next level. Thinks you disrespected him today."

"What are you talking about? I've trained him since he was a kid. I put years into him. And you're stealing him? And you helped him do this. You dishonest son-of-a-bitch! I took you in too!"

"That's the boxing business. I'll manage him and I'll train him. It's over, Jip".

Jip hung up the phone. He was despondent. He knew what was going to happen. Without Gideon there was no payday. The gym would close. All would be lost. Even worse is that he sold his soul to placate Gideon. He allowed a bully into the gym to spit at him, curse at him and disrespect him. He knew all along that this was a mistake as others saw it too and lost respect for him. And then he put his pride and joy, Noki, in the ring with a killer only to have him get hurt by cheating. For what? He risked everything and he now had nothing.

As he looked out of the window to the outside, mostly blocked by the shades, he could see one large shining star. For a while he just stared and then he began to pray. Jip was not a religious man and he was not praying to any god, just to the universe, to anything "out there" that could help him. First, he spoke to his wife and begged her forgiveness. Then he spoke to the star.

"Please help me. Please help us. I don't have much time left in this world. I only wish that whatever happens that my son, Noki, is taken care of. Please give my boy a real life."

There was no answer. No phone call. No epiphany. Only silence. After a while he dried his face and closed the lights to the gym as he went to the house. Bug was already resting in the janitor's closet waiting for Noki to come down and train later. Jip washed up and went to bed. He was not feeling well. He fed his fish, petted his cat and fell to sleep.

Chapter Twelve

The next morning, the knock on Bug's door was much more frantic than ever before. He knew something was wrong. He started to get his clothes on when the frantic knock came again. He hopped over with one leg out of his sweatpants and there was Noki, visibly shaken.

"What's wrong?"

"Come."

Bug put his other sweat pant leg on and then slipped on his sneakers. Noki was impatient and grabbed him by the wrist similar to the first time they met. He rushed Bug through the connector from the gym to the main house and then into Jip's room. There Jip lied, unable to speak and barely moving his limbs. Bug immediately grabbed the phone and called 911. He tried to calm Noki but Noki was rocking back and forth in the chair. He had no expression on his face but was obviously worried and shaken. Bug also called Limpy and told him to get to the park and tell the fighters that Jip is ill. He also gave him instructions to run the gym.

Over thirty minutes went by before the ambulance came. Bug waited for them outside to arrive. When they got there he was asked a myriad of questions about Jip by one of the rescue team members. The other was getting vital signs and trying, to no avail, to communicate with Jip. Bug really knew nothing of Jip's medical history. He later found out he had high blood pressure that he never did anything with.

This led to the stroke that was causing his sudden paralysis. The stress from the phone call, the night before, sure didn't help either but no one knew about that yet.

At the hospital Jip was put into intensive care after the ER evaluation. Noki and Bug stayed the whole time as the day led into night and then the morning. Luckily, Noki could drive them back and forth to the house. That was critical in this time because Bug's physical limitations made it hard for him to drive at all. In the past he could jimmy-rig a car with blocks taped to the pedals and a pillow or two on the seat so he could see out the windshield. Noki made that part unnecessary.

A few days went by and the prognosis was getting poorer for a full recovery. Life was not going to be the same for Noki, Bug or Carlo's Gym.

After a week, Jip was finally stabilized and was transferred to a step-down unit. His speech was so slurred it was impossible to understand him. His right side of his body was completely useless. The rehab team was now involved and after another week he was again transferred to a regular room, but his progression had slowed down. The stroke had taken its toll.

All during this time Bug and Jip would go back and forth to the gym to help out. The crowd there was thinning out. After Gideon left there was an exodus of fighters who no longer wanted to train there. They took their services to the gym across town where Gideon and John were now training. Bug had no doubt that John had a hand in this. For those who stayed, Limpy was able to help out. He proved to be trustworthy, which was critical during this type of crisis.

During the third week ,the doctors came out of Jip's room and told Noki and Bug that Jip would need long term SNF or skilled nursing facility residence.

"For how long?" Bug asked.

"I don't know. If he starts to improve then maybe he can go home someday but to be brutally honest, it's unlikely," the doctor told them.

"How do you know?"

"The CT scan shows that a major portion of his brain was damaged. Add to this that is rehab is progressing so slowly and you have a poor chance of recovery. I'm sorry to tell you this."

Noki and Bug went into the room after the doctors left. Bug tried to tell Jip how things were going. He decided not to tell him about Gideon because he was afraid it would upset him. Little did he know that Jip knew everything. Bug tried to be positive and explained how Limpy and Noki and he were taking care of the place. Jip would stare and barely move his head to acknowledge the comments. When Noki came to see him it was almost complete silence. Almost. "Come home, Papa", Noki said. There was nothing from Jip except a tear.

It was then that a strange visitor came into the room.

"Are you Bug?" he asked.

"Yes".

"And this must be Noki?"

Noki shook his head.

"Come with me."

CHAPTER THIRTEEN

They met in a conference room in the hospital. The woman had a pale blue pantsuit on. She was a heavy set, African -American woman in her mid-40s who just seemed out of place in this hospital environment. Her smile and overall pleasant demeanor was a breath of fresh air in what was a depressing place. She even had a glow about her.

"My name is Fay and I am the social worker in charge of your Dad's care".

Noki shook his head and said, "Okay". This was another rare time of Noki speaking up. He must have felt an innate connection with Fay as he did when he met Bug.

"What I have figured out so far is that Jip took care of you, Noki, and that Bug, well, you work there?"

"Yes, ma'am", Bug replied.

"And, Noki, your real name is Tyrone Polendina, son of Giuseppe "Jip" Polendina?"

"Yes, ma'am", Noki said copying Bug's reply.

"Okay, so here is where it gets tough. The doctor must have told you that Jip needs to go to a skilled nursing facility, correct?"

"Yes", said Bug. "Is that a good thing?"

"Going home would be a good thing. I hope eventually that will happen. Jip is going to a skilled nursing facility but it is only temporary to see if he gets better. If he can't take care of himself then they will end their attempts at trying and he moves on".

"To where?"

"That's the tough part. If you can't take care of him, which you would need endless amounts of money to equip your place and get extra help to care for him, then he would go to a permanent facility and basically get swallowed up by the system".

'Wait, I don't think we have the money for that", said Bug.

"Nobody really does. Medicare may pay some but Jip doesn't have a supplemental so he would get stuck with twenty percent of a massive bill. Actually, this hospitalization may cost him, and you, a lot.", Fay said.

"You mean that we may have to find some money to pay for all this? And to get him out of the system? We have to save him from all this? A dwarf and an autistic man-child?" Bug kept asking.

"Yeah, that doesn't seem likely. But maybe he'll get better? I am not a doctor" replied Fay.

"This is not good, Noki, but we'll be okay," Bug said as he turned to his friend.

"Hold on, Bug. There is some more bad news. I really represent the state and Noki, having his own issues, makes this complicated. He was adopted by Jip, we see that in the records, but he also gets a disability check due to his issues. This makes us wonder whether he needs to be taken back in by the system as well."

"I'll take care of him" Bug replied.

"Well, Bug, we don't even know who you are. My quick search can't even find your real name. You can see why we can't just give you Noki and everything Jip owns to take care of, right?"

"You can trust me."

"My sense is that I can, but it may not be up to me. Who are you really?"

"I'd rather not go into it", said Bug.

"Well, you kind of have no choice. I want to help you guys but I need information. It's up to you but…."

"My name is Jim Grillo and I was adopted, too. I am a vagabond. I have been everywhere. I have been used and abused. I've done anything I could do just to survive. I was also in the system as a foster child, but no one ever adopted me. Guess I didn't have any special talents. Anyway, I'll protect Noki and we will find a way to not let Jip get swallowed up in this system".

"Jip is not there yet. And neither is Noki. We just have some work to do. Listen, I'm on your side. Think of me as your Godmother here. I don't want to break anyone up. I want you all together, even with Jip. But I need to trust you. You can't lie to me, Bug."

"I won't".

"Ever."

"We promise"

"Both of you will also need to be brave and unselfish during these tough times. I really have no idea how you two will make it on your own, but I am here for you."

"We're fine".

"Do you have enough money?"

"Plenty", Bug replied.

"So, you are lying already?"

"We have money", said Noki. Bug was stunned that Noki again spoke up and at what he said.

"I sure hope you're telling the truth, Noki."

"I am", said Noki.

"Okay, then, well......the system is slooooowwwwwww. You have some time to figure things out. Bug, you need to fill this paperwork out so I can do my research and justify you being Noki's temporary guardian. Do not leave here without filling this out."

"Okay", Bug replied.

"Will you visit us again?" asked Noki.

"That's what Godmothers do", Fay said and smiled in a motherly manner.

CHAPTER FOURTEEN

On the drive home, Bug started to speak out loud as if he was speaking to Noki but he was really just trying to get his thoughts together. There was a lot to process.

"Noki, we are going to be all right, but we have a lot of work to do. We have to pray that Jip gets better, but if he doesn't then we have to take care of ourselves".

Noki nodded in agreement as he drove.

"We have to figure how much money Jip has and pay expenses. We have to get that gym up and running. If we can do that and prove to Fay that the state doesn't need to help us, then we are all set".

Noki kept nodding.

"You think we can pull this off?"

"Sure, I do," Noki said confidently.

Bug laughed. His good mood later went sour when he tried to decipher and organize what was going on in Jip's office. The place was a mess with paperwork everywhere. No one went into Jip's office unless they had business with him. Though Bug had started to gain Jip's confidence while apprenticing with him, he never was given full access to everything. No one really felt the need to keep Jip accountable. This had become a scavenger hunt and, luckily, Noki had

Jip's keys for the safe and file cabinets. There was no computer to break into, as Jip was technologically averse, which made things a little easier but not by much.

Bug spent the better part of the day trying to piece everything together while Limpy and Noki made sure the gym ran smoothly. He opened every bank statement, every message, every hand written note by a fighter promising to pay, etc. It wasn't until Noki came down to do his own late-night session did Bug feel comfortable in his knowledge of their financial situation.

"Noki, we need to talk", Bug said to Noki as he was about to start training. Noki went into the Jip's office with Bug.

"I'm pretty good at math. I know money. I'm not great at saving it but I know money. It comes with taking care yourself and living on nothing your whole life. Anyway, I looked at your dad's finances and, well, we're broke. "

Noki's head dropped.

"There are some overdue bills for electric and water. I can't get into the Jip's personal or business bank account, but it doesn't matter since the statements are all here and they are tapped. There isn't any money in there. He does own this gym and house, but he has a second mortgage on them and hasn't paid that in three months. We are done for. I do see that those disability checks for you were cashed but don't know where that went. This place cannot sustain itself. It's over."

Noki nodded his head no.

"Sorry, but yes."

Noki just kept nodding no.

"Yes, we are broke. Why do you keep disagreeing?"

Noki grabbed Bug's wrist again and walked him into the house and up to his room. Behind the large box of videotapes in his closed was a small container. Noki pulled out a large wade of cash.

"For us," Noki said.

"That's all your money, if we fail then you lose it all."

"For us".

Bug sat and counted the money. It was a about $4700. It obviously was some allowance that Jip was giving Noki from his disability checks and Noki never spent anything.

"This will last us two months, maybe three. We have no way of surviving after that. The gym doesn't really bring in much. And as far as I can tell, Jip doesn't even pay Limpy. He paysme next to nothing. This place has been running on fumes for a while. It's all smoke and mirrors. He truly was banking on Gideon because the other boxers bring in nothing. Unless you a have a long-term plan then we need to fess up to Fay because we have no plan."

They sat quietly together thinking. There was no talking. Finally, Bug spoke up, "There has to be a way to make money in this sport?"

"I can fight," Noki said.

"There is no way I can do that. It would kill Jip if you got hurt or hurt others and there is no way to guarantee that in this sport."

"Yes, there is," Noki responded and with that he reached for his tapes. He put in a one that Bug had not seen before. It looked like a knockout reel. In fact, he couldn't figure out why Noki was showing it to him. Every winning fighter on the tape was a different person getting the victory. It was until about the fifth fight that Bug realized that the loser was always the same person. That person was Bruce "The Mouse" Strauss. He was known as a professional loser. He would fake getting knocked out to get a payday. He fought his brother, he fought as his brother and he even fought twice in one night under two different names. He ruse was later found out, but it never bothered him. It was how he made a living. He even made fun of himself and bragged that he was "probably the only boxer in history that has lost by knockout on every continent."

"Why are you showing me this?

"Me", Noki pointed to himself.

"You want to get knocked out?"

"Not for real", Noki replied.

Noki had Bug stand up and coaxed him to throw a slow-motion punch his way. Bug did. With that Noki wobbled around the room as if he had been hit with a sledgehammer. That's when Bug got it. Noki could imitate anyone, even a professional loser ike "The Mouse".

Things haven't changed much since The Mouse fought. Boxing is so poorly run with such poor oversight that fighters could go from state to state and be professional opponents without anyone knowing. This is especially true when the fights aren't televised, which most aren't. Noki could lose on purpose and guarantee not to get hurt. Everyone would be happy. And they would make money because opponents are needed to build up the records of up-and-coming boxers. In fact, many times the opponents get more money because of this. And that is what Bug and Noki could do. It wasn't a great plan but at least it was a plan. Now they needed to find someone to help them with this.

"Frankie Calzone is who you want," said Limpy the next day.

"I saw his name in Jip's book", said Bug, "Who is he?"

"He is one of those slimy fight guys that does this kind of thing. He can take Noki and get his name out there to be used as a loser. You sure you won't get the kid hurt?"

"Tap him on the chin", Bug told Limpy.

Limpy slowly slapped Noki on his chin and Noki wobbled and took a swan dive to the ground as if he was just shot.

"Yeah, he won't get hurt", said Limpy, "Okay, Calzone, is who you need. Just don't trust him."

"I get it, I don't trust anybody, but we have no choice", said Bug.

Chapter Fifteen

Enormous would be the best way to describe Frank Calzone. Bug and Noki went to meet him at a construction site. The large trailer, which was his office, leaned down in the back right corner, exactly where Calzone sat doing business or when playing cards with the boys. And that is what he did all day, every day.

Bug knocked on the door to the trailer and he heard Calzone's booming voice asking him to come in. The smell of cigars and body odor was unbearable.

"Boys", said Calzone to two other card players, "Looks like I have some business".

The other men stared down Bug and Noki as they walked out.

"Sit", Calzone, "Limpy told me about you".

"How do you know Limpy?"

"In boxing everyone knows everyone."

"Well, did he explain our dilemma?"

"Yeah, you want to make some money being a tomato can?"

"What?" asked Bug.

"A professional loser."

"Yes, Noki is really good at this and can make it…."

"I don't give a shit about what he can or cannot do. What he has to do is make it a close enough fight to fool people and then get knocked out."

"He can do that".

"Great. If the kid can fight why don't you just let him fight?"

"We don't want him hurt."

"Listen, what's your name?"

"Bug."

"Listen, Buck…"

"It's Bug."

"Bug, Buck, who gives a shit? Boxing is a hurt business. Anyone could get hurt. If he is good, I could get him some real fights here and there."

"Could we make money?"

"Maybe in a year or two when his record is really good. No one is going to pay good money for him to build up his record."

"We don't have that much time."

"Then he needs to be a loser and I can arrange that. You came to the right place".

Bug was not so sure, but he had no choice. "Is there a contract?" he asked.

"A contract?", Calzone started to laugh, "Look at this fucking guy?" he responded to no one. "You'll get paid. I work with the promoters. They need stiffs. They will pay you after the fight and then you'll pay me a third."

"A third?"

"Don't like it? Then get the fuck out!"

"Will they pay?"

"If you listen to me and do what I just said."

"When can he start?"

"There is a fight in Oklahoma Saturday. What is he, a light heavyweight?"

"Yes, umm, I think. I'm not sure", Bug guessed.

"How much do you weigh?" Calzone asked Noki with no response, "Can he understand? Hooowwww muccccchhhh doooo yoooouuuu weighhhhh?"

"He's not deaf. He's speaks English. And he's not slow. He's autistic".

"You mean he can paint too?

63

"Not artistic. Autistic, he doesn't process things like we do but he is all there."

"As long as he processes the fact that he needs to lose then I'm fine. I have Jip's office number and I will call you with more details. If this works out, I can get a couple of fights a week for you. Different states. You would need to get a few different names to put on a few different boxing licenses."

"What?"

"Well, you'll need a legitimate license to start. But they ain't going to let him get knocked out every time and continue. We have to mix it up and keep them guessing. "

"Is this legal?"

"I love this fucking guy", Calzone laughed as looked to get acknowledgment from others in the room, but again, no one was there. "You need money. He needs money. I can set this up so you can make me money. Does that sound illegal to you?"

"Well…"

"Now get out. I have to take a shit."

That scared Noki and Bug more than anything they had heard in the past twenty minutes. As they rushed out the door, they could feel the trailer shift as Calzone began to get out of his seat.

"You sure want to do this?" Bug asked Noki.

"Yes", Noki responded, "We need the money".

"But it's not worth it if you get hurt."

"I won't get hurt" Noki smiled as he responded.

Bug wasn't as confident. Playing around in the gym is one thing. Doing it in a real fight is another.

CHAPTER SIXTEEN

Their first fight was in Austin, Texas. Noki weighed 174 pounds. His opponent was a decent up-and-coming light heavyweight fighter from the local area with a record of 4-0. At the weigh-ins he tried to intimidate Noki with some choice words and a stare down. This is a common technique used by fighters and it works much of the time. Such tactics did not affect Noki. Nothing bothered him, in fact. His inability to pick up social cues was now a positive. In fact, it may have had a reverse effect on his opponent.

The local fans were there for their guy and the promoter set it up so that he and Noki were the main event. This is unusual to have a fighter, Noki, who had never fought pro or amateur before, be the main event. That's because it wasn't about Noki but about their guy and making his fans happy. Noki and Bug decided he should fight in the style of Pernell Whitaker so as not to get hurt. "Sweat Pea" Whitaker fought mostly in the 80s and 90s was a four-weight world champion (lightweight, light welterweight, welterweight, and light middleweight). He was also a southpaw, which means he fought as a lefty. Pernell was an outstanding fighter and counterpuncher, which meant he would wait for your punch to punch back. Noki and Bug had watched him over and over again in their time together and they thought it would be perfect for this fight.

The fans were expecting a blowout but instead saw an artist show off his skill. And it wasn't their guy. Noki was fighting lefty and tagging the local favorite with jabs and body punches after slipping the other guy's shots. Bug was amazed. This kid could mimic anyone, even changing his dominant hand from righty to lefty. There was so much confidence and so much talent in his movements. He literally transformed himself into Sweat Pea. This also meant he was killing the guy on points and any real judge should have seen that. This started to worry Bug between the third and fourth round because there was only one round left. Noki had to lose to get paid. He was not there to beat anyone in this crooked game. In the final round Noki continued his strategy. The opponent started swinging wildly and missing wildly. The guy knew he was in trouble, but he was fatigued and that is when Noki took advantage, but not to finish him but to get finished. A weak right hand slightly grazed Noki's left temple. There was nothing on the punch but Noki made it look like he was hit with a ton of bricks. First his right leg shook and then his left knee hit the ground. The referee immediately came over and started to count. Noki got up on the count of 8 and motioned to the ref he was ready to continue but wobbled so much that the ref called the fight off. The other fighter went crazy with joy. The ring doctor took a look at Noki and cleared him of anything major as the fans were standing and screaming. Their local hero won again. Noki was now 0-1 and would get paid nicely when he left the arena.

On the ride home Bug asked, "You enjoyed it in there, didn't you?"

Noki nodded his head yes as he drove. And he started to smile

"Well, I am proud of you. You really are something special. The knockout looked great. Did you get hurt?"

Noki smiled and shook his head no.

"Would you rather have won?"

"Yes," Noki said.

"Well, we can't let you do that. They don't pay the winners unless they have a great record and fight in the big fights. We both heard that. Do you understand?"

Noki nodded yes.

"Besides, the only goal is to make money and that is what we are doing. Limpy is trying to get more fighters to come to the gym so it can sustain itself. He is looking at bringing in more white-collar, regular people to teach them. It's a new workout fad for lawyers and brokers and whatever. He said Jip wanted no part of it, but we are stuck. Besides those people are nicer and may pay their dues."

Again, Noki nodded. Bug sat on a telephone book so he could see out of the windshield. "We'll just keep this going for a while and see where it takes us."

The next day they met up at Frankie Calzone's trailer, gave him the money in the envelope he received from the promotor and Frank paid them about $700.

"I thought we were getting close to a $1000 for these fights?" Bug asked forgetting all the details of their verbal contract.

"You did. The rest is my fee. You don't like it then get the fuck out," Calzone aggressively responded."

"Okay, sorry, we need the money. And more fights."

"Well, your boy did well. I got another fight tonight for you in east Texas. Can he do it?"

"Sure."

"Have him start growing his hair longer and not shave so he gets a full beard. "

"Why?"

"Eventually he is going to have to look different and then we can have him shave it down to a mustache and then later shave it all off including his head. It's all about fooling people so he can continue the charade."

"Okay, I get it. He's a puppet and you're his puppet master."

"What? You don't like that? Then…."

"Get the fuck out, yes, I get it, I get it", replied Bug

"Now you are starting to understand. It's only a matter a time before you get caught by someone and then you'll be banned."

"How long?"

"Can't say. There's a lot of stupid and crooked people in this business who couldn't care less. Not many dwarfs running around the sport as trainers either. You'd think they would figure it out but they're idiots. That being said, when one rat spills the beans you're done."

"We will be extra careful", Bug said as he and Noki walked out. They felt the trailer shake again and knew that Frankie was ready to do his own business in the bathroom again.

CHAPTER SEVENTEEN

The fight in East Texas was in a sleazy town. Their local hero was 7-1 and twenty pounds heavier than Noki. This time Noki fought with the style of Benny Leonard. They thought it would be fun and different. Leonard was born Benjamin Leiner and is considered by many to be in the top ten boxers of all time. He held the lightweight title for eight years (1917-1925) and was known for his speed and reflexes. His style was different than fighters of the present era as he was more straight up and bounced around, pulling his head back each time. Noki copied it all, even the extended and half-straightened left arm that he used for jabs. The fight was boring as Noki beautifully slipped punches or blocked them with his right glove. He actually caught the guy in the second round with a hard shot and hurt him. The local hero actually fell into Noki's arms because he was hit lunging forward. Noki held him up and wrestled around with him a little to keep him standing. The fans were getting restless, and nervous, until a few seconds later when their fighter awkwardly threw a left hook. Noki blocked with his right hand but he pretended it hurt him anyway. Once again, his knees wobbled and the next punch was a right cross, which Noki slipped by spinning his head with the punch. There was no damage but Noki went down like a lump of clay.

After the fight, and after they were paid by the promoter, Noki and Bug walked out to go home. They were greeted by drunk fans who began to mock Bug's size and call Noki things like "fucking loser" or "glass chin pussy" or worse. Bug was getting annoyed and pushed Noki through the crowd and in towards the car. A few fans outside continued the verbal barrage. Bug was amazed how simple and naïve people can be. He saw it in his past life. Different people, same behavior. It sure doesn't making losing any better, even when you do it on purpose. That's how Bug felt, at least, but Noki didn't show any emotion. He was the picture of stoicism, which probably was his autism and not a practiced skill. Or maybe it was?

This drive home was different. Bug once again was using the telephone book and two wooden blocks to drive the vehicle on the long trip home. Noki slept most of the way while Bug's mind wandered. He wasn't excited that Noki was becoming a paid loser. Itjust didn't feel right having him fight with these strings attached. There were some positives, though. He was actually winning both fights handily against pretty good fighters and this was getting him great experience. But for what? At least he was not letting Noki get hurt or hurt others and that is what he felt he owed to Jip. There was good money to be made this way but what Bug was worried about what would happen if situation gets noticed? Would there be trouble, more than being suspended or getting his license pulled? Bug had no idea. And what about Fay, the social worker? What would she think?

The scenario played out similarly for the next few weeks. They were getting two fights per weekend. The most tiring thing was the long drives to these out of the way fighting arenas. Sometimes they rotated driving. Sometimes they didn't come home and just slept in the car instead. Each time Noki, out of boredom, would switch styles of great defensive fighters. One night it was James Toney, the next it was Marco Antonio Barrera. Another weekend he was Roberto Duran and the next it was Marvin Hagler. The most recent weekend he fought like Winky Wright and then Roy Jones, Jr. There was no fighter he could not imitate. Each fight he held punches back to make sure he was not in a position to get hit but still made the fight close. Each knockout was as theatrical as the next.

During the week they would visit Jip who now was in another facility over 40 minutes away. They never told him what Noki was doing for fear of effecting his recovery, which was painfully slow. It was evident that there was a chance he could never come home. That was heartbreaking for both of them and obviously took an emotional toll on Noki. He would not drive the vehicle home from those visits and would not communicate with Bug in the car back to the house. Bug was noticing this more and more. Jip's cat stayed with Noki now and the goldfish was moved up to his room as well. Noki still would box on his own at night and then watch films with Bug before bed. This is also how he prepared for his next style of fighting.

By the third month he was officially 0-7 with all losses by knockouts. The other five fights were under a different name, so it was actually 0-12. None of the fights were televised so no one had proof of anything other than the record under his own name. Unfortunately, it was enough for the Texas Boxing Commission to call the gym and speak with the person in charge. Bug was on the phone for over an hour and got nowhere. Their dictum was non-negotiable. To their credit they were not going to let a fighter keep getting knocked out.

He was not allowed to fight for another month and if he got knocked out again, he would be permanently suspended with his license pulled. This didn't affect other state commissions as information wasn't shared between them but it sure would put a damper on their plan. Bug called Calzone who laughed and said, "Well, it was a good run." Bug and Noki were headed back into financial trouble. And Jip was still not coming back anytime soon and it didn't matter if he did. It became obvious to them that they weren't going to pull the Bruce "The Mouse" Strauss trick anymore and since the gym was still not supporting itself, troubling times were ahead. The good news was that Limpy was getting a few white-collar boxers there to teach lessons to but not nearly enough.

A few days after Noki's last fight a visitor came to the gym. A familiar face but a dishonest one.

"I want to help you guys out", John said. It was his first visit back since Jip had his stroke.

"How would you like to do that?" asked Bug.

"Well, you know that Gideon is now the holder of one of the smaller belts and is number one in the world. His title shot is three months away and he'll win it."

"I heard".

"Gideon wants to buy the place. He just feels more comfortable here. He'll take the house too. You all would have to go."

"Why would we do that?"

"Because you have no money. It's going to go under. You can get some cash to go live in an apartment with the retarded kid. Get him some toys to chew on."

"You're an asshole, you know that? He's not retarded. He's autistic. You've been here long enough that you should know that. Besides, I would never sell to you or Gideon anyway. I'd rather burn the place first. More importantly, I don't own it. Jip does and he can't give that decision."

"Well, that's too bad. Maybe we need to do what it takes to make this happen?"

"What does that mean?"

"It's a small world, this boxing business. I know about your little theatrical games you're playing with the kid. He's an actor now. What if the word got out that you're using him to make money and he's getting hurt because of it?"

"But he's not getting hurt."

"Oh, I know. I know he is faking his knockouts. But you can't admit that to anyone or you'll go to jail for fraud. Both of you. So, you will have to go with the story of him actually trying but he is just not good enough and you're letting people pummel this retard's melon. You see how this would play out in the press? Heck, the state may want to take him now because of it."

"You son-of-a-bitch".

"Hey, that's life. That's boxing. You played your little game but it's over. Figure a way to sell us this place."

"I told you, I don't own it."

"Gideon doesn't care. I don't care. He starts his next training camp in six weeks and wants to do it here. What Lionel Gideon wants, Lionel Gideon gets. Figure a way."

John left the gym and Bug sat in the office for hours trying to figure things out. He couldn't. As Noki started his late-night training Bug looked out the office window and saw a large shining star in the distance. The same one Jip prayed to, though Bug didn't know that.

"Well, I'm not a person that really wishes for anything but if someone can help us then please, please help show me a way out of this mess. This kid is the definition of goodness and just wants to be here and do his thing. Why is everything and everyone against him? Please give me a hint."

Bug walked out of the office, looked at his pocket watch, and saw Noki come in to work out. It was 10:02 PM again. This time Bug wasn't really paying attention to Noki as he was lost in thought. He knew he had to talk to someone who could help him. Someone who cared and may actually be on their side. But who? That's when it hit him.

CHAPTER EIGHTEEN

"You all did what!?"

"Please don't yell. Noki will get scared". Noki was still smiling in the seat next to Bug, obviously enamored with Fay. He wasn't scared at all.

"You did what?" Fay repeated in a softer voice.

"Like I said, we needed to make some money to keep the place going. We had no choice."

"Doesn't this gym business make money?"

"No. Jip left the finances in shambles. He put a lot of money in this kid Lionel Gideon. Paid for his condo, his meals, his everything and let everything else go by the wayside. "

"So, why haven't you just stopped paying for him?"

"Well, we did because he left us. Now there is very little left, and we were down to Noki's own personal money to keep us afloat".

"And your only plan was to put Noki out there as bait to get beat up? Are you kidding me!?"

"First, it isn't our only plan. We have a trainer, Limpy, who is trying to make the gym more upscale with white-collar fighters. You know, doctors and lawyers and such. He gets paid to be their personal trainer and we get their monthly dues."

"And how is that going?"

"Well, he has two clients."

"So not good."

"No, not good."

"And no other ideas?"

"Yes, Noki's idea. He knew that he could make us some money by getting knocked out and still not getting hurt."

"Why would they pay the losers more money?"

"Boxing is crooked. They use stiffs, bodies, tomato cans or whatever you call them to build up records of up and coming fighters."

"What, there is no national organization that watches over this?"

"Nope. There are some "world" organizations but it is so poorly run that anyone could be a fighter and make some money by losing. Only Noki can do it, though, by not getting hurt."

"Why Noki?"

"Because Noki is a great fighter". Noki smiled and patted Bug on the back.

"Yes, I appreciate you flattering him, but we need to have an honest discussion here. I need the truth, Bug".

"Listen, I am not a boxing trainer. I am more of a fan than I ever was thanks to the hundreds of hours of boxing film Noki has made me watch. Here's what I know, this kid is an awesome boxer."

"He's been knocked out....how many times?"

"12".

"Twelve times....wait, what? I thought his record is 0-7".

"Well, he fought under a few different names. Long story."

"How unregulated is this sport? My God. No one can figure out that this is the same fighter? He has a little person in his corner. That can't be a common thing. And listen to what you just told me. You have been driving Noki around to get knocked out between 7 and 12 times".

"12"

"Whatever, twelve times, and you did this because losers make more money as opponents. So, in reality, his record is 0-12 with all knockouts".

"Yes."

"But....but...you are telling me that Noki is a great fighter."

"More than great. Maybe the best ever". Noki smiled again and patted Bug on the head.

"Stop doing that," Fay told Noki, "What the hell are you talking about?" she asked Bug.

"There is something different about Noki?"

"Obviously. He's autistic."

"I know. But more than that. He has this photographic memory when he watches boxing film or watches fighters. He somehow can take information and then transfer that into his own physical skills. He becomes them with their moves. I can't explain it."

"The old term, the bad term, was idiot savant. Now it's called autistic savant. I have seen them do math, do sculptures and play music so I guess anything is possible. I have never seen it transferred into a physical sport before. Wait, so why are you letting him lose?" asked Fay.

"Well, that's the thing. It was about the money. He really just loves fighting like a dancer loves dancing. He doesn't care about winning or losing. Well, if he had his choice he would like to win but there is no ego in Noki. He's not like the rest of us. Losing got us more cash and he didn't need to risk getting hurt by trying to win. That would have exposed him to more punches. Also, no one would have paid him much until his record was good enough to get noticed. They say that takes years."

"This is all too confusing for me. Okay, Noki is losing and that makes you money. He is a savant and could be or is a great fighter. So, why are you here?"

"That's the rub. The commission suspended him for a month. They think he is 0-7 with seven losses by KO. Now we can try to fight out of state for a bit but that is going to run dry quick. Also, that fighter, Lionel Gideon, who Jip spent all his money on, had a big win and will probably win the title in a few months. He wants our gym and house and offered a ridiculous low amount."

"That's Jip's house. No one could sell it but him unless he perishes and then Noki can, but I am not even sure about that."

"I understand. That is why I am here. I can't figure a way out of this. Gideon's trainer is a lowlife and is going to tell the media and the state and anyone else he can find that we are abusing and exploiting an autistic young man."

"Yeah, that's going to be a problem. But you did well in coming here because it would have come back to me at some point because I am in charge of this case. "

"So?"

"So what? I don't have answers for you. It seems to me that Noki can't get 'knocked' out any more. That does look bad and so it isn't an option. I guess if he was doing the knocking out then my defense would be to say that he is winning and why shouldn't we let an autistic person fight? Especially if he is winning?"

81

"That will work?"

"I have no idea. All I know is that the state, who is my boss, can't let him get hurt. But if he is not getting hurt then this may end up being a legal and ethical battle that could last a while. It may give you enough time for you to make some money. But you said that would take time to get to the point where he makes that money?"

"That is what I have been told. I need to see what options are out there for him. But you're saying winning would buy him time?" asked Bug

"I think. Better than getting knocked out will."

"Time is what we need. I need to talk to some people. Hey, Noki, do you still want to fight?"

Noki smiled and nodded his head.

"Do you understand what we have been saying here?"

Noki nodded yes.

"Do you want to win now?"

"Yes, I want to win," he said. Noki's face lit up. He stood up and hugged Fay.

"Bug," Fay said as she finished with Noki's embrace, "I am trusting you with this boy. I don't like boxing. I don't want him hurt. You're his conscience. Promise me you will stop this if he gets in over his head."

"I promise."

CHAPTER NINETEEN

"What do we do now Frankie?" Bug asked.

"Well, the kid can't get knocked out anymore. That's for sure. I'm not even sure he can have another loss on his record. But I may be able to make this work", Frank Calzone responded.

"How? You said if Noki wins he wouldn't get any more fights".

"Fughetaboutit. With all these losses on his record they won't know he isn't a tomato can."

"And that will work?"

"For a while, until they figure him out. But your boy needs to win or the commission will shut him down. He can win, right?"

"Yes", Bug replied and then turned his head to the man-child, "Noki, can you win?"

"Yes." Noki said.

"That will piss these local promotors off", said Calzone, "That will piss them off a lot. You need to get your money quickly and get the hell out of there. That is if they pay you at all. Some will stiff you and ,even worse, hurt you".

"How do we make money then?"

"I am going to bet on you. You know, underground betting. Everyone will be betting on their local hero. Vegas doesn't give a shit about small time boxing so I have to use bookies. No one locally will believe an 0-7 fighter with seven KO losses can actually fight. He can fight, right?"

"Yes, he can fight!" Bug repeated.

"Great, I can make some bets on your kid here. If he wins, then I'll make some money".

"Ok, so you make some money but what about us?" Bug asked.

"What are you deaf? I just said you need to get paid and get the hell out of there!"

"So, we keep all the all the money from the actual fight this time? And you just make money betting?"

"Yes, it will be much cleaner that way. I'll call you when we find have a fight. Now, if you don't mind....".

"We know, get the fuck out. You have to take a shit."

"I love it. This is becoming a nice relationship."

Noki drove back home but they made a stop to see Jip again. This time they were more prepared. They had a VCR with them and a way to hook it up to the hospital television. Jip was able to watch some fights with both Bug and Noki. Jip could shake his head to answer but was still not very communicative verbally. Some words were coming but it was tough to understand most of them, which made him frustrated. His right side was still paralyzed and even getting him to sit up and watch was an extraordinary effort. There was some progress, however.

Noki was so happy to share this time with Jip like they did when he was a kid. Bug, on the other hand, was feeling guilty because he was unable to share with Jip what he was doing with his precious son. He was torn and came to the realization that this is what Jip probably was feeling when allowed Gideon to rule the gym and when he let Noki spar with Gideon. Bug was starting to understand the old man even more. It just didn't make things any easier.

CHAPTER TWENTY

"No!" Noki yelled.

"Let me just show you," replied Limpy.

"No. I like the VCR!".

"I can't get you the films for VCR anymore!" screamed Limpy.

"No."

"Calm down!" Bug yelled as he walked out of the office, "What's going on?"

"I have films of this kid from San Antonio. He's not bad. Noki should watch him but all I have is from YouTube. He has to hook a computer up to a TV."

"Noki, that sounds reasonable. We have some money right now. Let's get you better equipment."

"No. I love my tapes!"

"We're not taking the tapes from you. Or your VCR. They are yours forever. But now you can watch films with newer fighters. So, let's do what your dad always says, which is tend to business."

Noki cocked his head off to the distance staring at the corner of the gym, thought about it for about an awkward second and then smiled. "Okay", and he walked back to the locker room to help clean things up. Due to Noki's autism, he didn't often react like others. Once convinced, Noki's anger would leave and was gone forever. He never held a grudge. Well, almost never. Like many autistic people, he still could get hung up or fixated on certain objects, behaviors or routines. Most of the time, though, Noki just let the emotion go a like stick floating down the river. Almost all the sticks were gone for good.

"How good is this next kid, Limpy?" asked Bug.

"Good."

"Crap. We never really cared before. It was less nerve-wracking when you knew you were going to lose."

Limpy showed Bug a few of his fights from his phone. They were both impressed. The fight in San Antonio was not going to be an easy one. Their hyped local prospect was 8 and 0 and actually had some skills.

"Okay, how do we get this so Noki can watch it?" asked Bug.

"You need a television that can connect to the Internet and we just watch it on YouTube there."

"What about his tapes?"

"Just leave his television and system alone and we'll put the new TV right next to it."

"Great, here is some cash." Bug said giving Limpy a few hundred dollars, "Please try to get is as soon as you can."

"I'll go after training and be back here before 8 tonight," Limpy replied.

"Sounds good", replied Bug, who sought out Noki and asked him to come into the main office.

"Noki, tomorrow we have to start doing things differently, okay?"

"No."

"You haven't even heard what I was going to say."

"No changes."

"Well, I need you to win. I need you to train with a real trainer. I can't do it. Limpy has to be the guy and needs to do it after all the training is done at about 3 and so he can be ready for the white-collar boxers at 5.

Noki looked away for a while and there was a massive 6-second pause.

"Noki are you there? We can't even find sparring at 10 at night. You need to move your training up to 3 pm".

"What about my job? I clean."

"This is your job now. I can pitch in more for the cleaning. Maybe we make enough money someday to get some help.

There was now another 5-second pause as Noki thought about it and then said, "Yes. But not forever."

"Okay, deal, but we start tomorrow", Bug replied.

That night Limpy hooked everything up as Noki nervously stared at him. "It's going to be fine, Noki", Limpy said.

The three of them huddled in Noki's room and watched online video of the kid from San Antonio. Limpy was now becoming part of the team, which was great because Bug needed him. Bug had only entered the boxing world months ago. Limpy had years and years of experience. Bug was also not tall enough to hold the hand pads for Noki. Limpy even had some mediocre cutman skills just in case there were troubles during a fight. It was a no brainer to include him and the three of them were a sight to see: a little person, a disabled ex-fighter with a severe limp, and an autistic savant. They didn't look like a dream team but hopefully looks didn't matter.

After watching the video ,Noki went over to his collection and pulled out the tape of the person he decided to imitate. Joseph Louis Barrow, or Joe Louis, was one of the 100 greatest punchers of all time. He was world heavyweight champion from 1937 to 1949 and his nickname was the "Brown Bomber". He successfully defended his title 25 times! He was much more of an upright fighter with a great jab and powerful punches from both hands. He wasn't flashy and did not throw punches wildly. Louis liked to stalk fighters and do his damage from close range. He also could counterpunch and ,when he hit someone, they felt it.

"Works for me", Bug said, "How about you Limpy".

"Hell, yeah, homey." He replied.

The next day Noki walked in from the connector to his house and was already in his gear. He started his warm up just like many of the other fighters. Boxing gyms are not organized like other sports. They are not part of a team. Fighters complete their workout depending on their own plan or their trainer's plan, if they even have a trainer. Usually there is a warm-up followed by some bag work and then either sparring or hitting hand pads and then a cool down. It is still archaic with little changes over the past century. None of the fighters are doing the exact same thing as the other as they may start at different times or rotate to different areas at different times. Somehow this chaos works. Today was different.

This was Noki's first week training with them and everyone was surprised to see him. Since Gideon's leaving, only about a dozen fighters remained in the gym and most of them were amateurs. Only a few had seen him spar with Gideon so hardly anyone knew he had skills and no one had actually seen him practice before. They mostly just saw him cleaning up around the place. It was like they saw a ghost when Noki hopped up into the ring and started to shadow box with a few other boxers in there. They nodded their heads in acknowledgement as all of them just threw punches in the air. Noki did not nod back, a product of his inability to pick up these social cues.

As Noki trained that day, some of the other fighters were confused on how he was a different fighter than the one they saw sparring Gideon. On that day he was Willie Pep. Today, As Noki banged the bags or hit the hand pads that Limpy was holding, these boxers saw a totally different style. They were not knowledgeable about older fighters, so they didn't know it was Joe Louis he was imitating. What they did know, however, is that Noki was really good at what he was doing. Noki was working hard and hitting hard. His punches were crisp and powerful. The other fighters who saw him, even those that looked out of the corner of their eyes, were more than impressed. To Noki, however, it was just part of his game. He loved boxing. He loved the styles of great boxers. He loved acting like these fighters. It was like a kid who pretends to be Michael Jordan on the local basketball court or Tom Brady while playing touch football with his friends. This was his mental fantasy. This was his fun.

CHAPTER TWENTY-ONE

It was a warm Texas night in San Antonio. The arena was not far from the Riverwalk, where many of the locals drank and ate. On this night their local guy was ready to push his record to 8-0. As an amateur, Juan Mendez tore up the competition and reigned as state Golden Glove champion for the past three years. He skipped trying to make the Olympic team in an effort to push his pro career faster. One of his biggest appeals was his size. It was quite rare for a fighter of Mexican heritage to be a light heavyweight. He was also good looking, which made the women love him.

Noki was a replacement for another fighter who backed out at the last minute. This did not affect the crowd size. The local news team was ready to film highlights, but it was not a televised fight for cable or any other channel. Who would ever want to see an 8-0 fighter box a 0-7 fighter, especially with the former having knocked everyone out and the latter always getting knocked out?

After eight preliminary fights the crowd was getting hungry for their champ and for a gruesome knockout. The last preliminary match was going on as Noki, Bug and Limpy sat in the dressing room.

"Well, let's start warming up, Noki," Limpy told him.

Noki, already gloved, stood up and started to shadow box. That's when the promoter walked in.

"Listen, I need a fight here. These fans are crazy. Your kid may be terrible but make him last a few rounds, okay?"

Noki smiled but Bug only nodded. He was starting to worry about the fight more and more. What the hell was he doing here? Before their new plan, Noki was just trying to find a nice warm spot to fall onto when he pretended to get hit. Now it was for real. Now he had to win.

As time went on and the fight got closer, Noki moved on to hitting the hand pads that Limpy was holding. Bug looked at him and saw no sign of nerves. No sign of fear. It was absolutely amazing. Bug had already used the bathroom three times due to anxiety. Noki was just the opposite, calm and robotic. Then another man walked into the dressing room.

"I'm Will Brown from the Texas Boxing Commission. I'm not even sure how your kid got this fight or why someone at our office approved it, but I am here to warn you that I will petition to have his license permanently revoked if he loses, much less gets knocked out. This Mendez kid is good, so I am sure this is going to happen and happen quick, but I didn't want our suspension to come as a surprise to you later."

"Thanks for the pep talk, Will," Bug said, "Are you a professional motivational speaker in your day job?"

Will Brown smirked and turned and left. At that moment a fighter was being helped into the locker room. He had just been knocked cold and they were looking for a spot to put him. Bug had to get up to give them room. He almost had to use the bathroom another time when he saw another young staff man quickly open the door.

"Okay, fellas, you're on", said one of the staff working for the promoter.

Noki was gloved up with a decent pair of boxing shorts on and only a t-shirt covering his upper half. There was no fancy robe. His t-shirt had Dumbo on the front.

"Noki, remind me to get you another shirt next time," Bug said as they all walked to the ring. Noki didn't acknowledge the comment. He was 100% focused. As he entered the ring the fans booed him. Again, Noki paid no attention. Then they stood up and started to scream as Mendez walked towards the ring to the Mariachi music he had specifically chosen. It was called "No Me Se Rajar," which translates to "I don't know how to give up." This is a song Julio Cesar Chavez Sr., one of the best Mexican fighters ever, used for his fights. The fans loved it and they showed it by getting even rowdier.

As Mendez climbed through ropes, he smirked at Noki in a condescending manner. His cornermen helped him take off his beautiful robe as they dried him off and put Vaseline on his face. Noki, in the other corner, just bounced up and down staying warm. The fans laughed as the announcer told the crowd Noki's record. Bug was embarrassed, but once again, it didn't faze Noki. Then the crowd erupted when Mendez's information was rattled off.

They met in the center of the ring as the ref gave instructions. Mendez was smiling at Noki, staring into his eyes. Noki just stared back like he stares at his videotapes. Menendez's confidence was sky high, knowing he was fighting an 0-7 fighter. How could he not confident? He beamed at the crowd as he walked back to his corner to have his mouthpiece put in by his trainer. Noki, on the other hand, was stone-faced. When he went back to the corner Limpy put his mouthpiece in and Bug said, "Just like we talked about. Joe Louis against Max Schmeling. The second fight. Tend to business. Okay?" Noki nodded his head yes.

The bell rang and Noki immediately started to stalk Mendez. Mendez, an aggressive fighter himself, was stunned at this and tried to back Noki off with some big shots. All were blocked. Soon Noki had Mendez stuck in a corner and hammered him with a five-shot barrage. All but one hit its target. Mendez went down. It was only 23 seconds into the first round, The fans were shocked and now quiet. They could not believe their eyes. At the count of 8 he was up and that is when Noki threw almost 27 straight punches that had Mendez out on his feet. The fight was over halfway through the first round. You could hear a pin drop in the arena. The doctor took a look at Mendez as he was helped to his feet. As Noki was announced the winner, with the referee raising his hand, the fans booed and started to throw bottles into the ring. It was almost a riot.

Noki, Limpy and Bug scrambled out of the ring to their locker room. They quickly started to dress. There was no sign of the promoter. No sign of Will Brown, from the Texas Boxing

Commission. They were alone. And they waited and waited. The fans were about gone when the three moved into the arena to search for the promoter. They found him talking to some of the staff.

"Can we get our money?" asked Bug.

"Yeah," he reluctantly replied, "What the fuck was that?"

"Was what?"

"How did your guy pull this off?"

"He got lucky, I guess."

"It didn't look like a lucky punch? Something ain't right about this shit. I was just sold a bill of goods because that was bullshit."

"I'm confused. Why do you not want your fans to see a real fight with a real chance of the other guy winning?"

"Because this is about getting Mendez in a position for the big fight. He wasn't supposed to struggle in a bullshit local fight. He was my ticket to some big money. Someone pulled some shit on me and I think I know who that was."

Bug knew he was talking about Frank Calzone, but he didn't care. All he cared about was the money and he finally got some cash out of the promoter. The three of them moved towards the exit and then to their car. They were not easy to miss due to the quirkiness of the three but luckily most of the fans had left. When they got to the car, they saw all the beer bottles broken on it with dents everywhere and their windshield smashed. Luckily it was still drivable as they got in and made the trip home.

"Well, with all the damage to the car and our expenses for the trip we didn't make as much as we wanted."

"Boxing is still the wild west, homey", replied Limpy, "But at least Noki won. Great job, Noki."

Noki smiled.

"This is not going to be an easy journey," Bug replied.

"You mean this drive?" asked Limpy

"No, I mean this kid's career", said Bug

"No, my man, it's not going to be easy", Limpy answered as they started the three hour trip home.

CHAPTER TWENTY-TWO

"Well, you have another fight in a small Louisiana town next weekend", said Calzone.

"Why so soon?" asked Bug.

"I thought you needed the money", Calzone replied.

"Yeah, we do. But a week?"

"Look at this fucking guy", Calzone said this time to the two other guys at the card table in the trailer. "Listen, the word will get out quickly. This won't last."

"Word?" asked Bug.

"That your kid is a ringer. That his record don't mean shit and that he can fight. Then they won't risk their own local dumbass' record anymore."

"Then what?"

"Then you're fucked."

The following week the team studied the online videos of Ragin' Cajun Broussard. He was a cagey fighter with good power. His record was 10-1 and his only loss was by a cut. After seeing as much as they could on YouTube, Noki reached for one of his videotapes and put it on. It was a highlight reel of Oscar De La Hoya. His reign lasted from the 1990s to the late 2000s and he held six world title belts. Oscar was an incredible technical fighter with a great jab. He had great footwork and defense but could punch to the body and head with equal success. He could stay out of his opponent's range but then jump on his fighter with lethal combinations. This was who Noki needed to be to in order to frustrate and beat Broussard.

By this time, Noki, Bug and Limpy were used to the routine. They were treated poorly when they came to town. They were ridiculed at the morning weigh-in and laughed at when they left. At night they had the "losers" locker room where all the other "opponents" were lined up. It almost harkened back to the Roman gladiators where the soon to be killed were kept in one area while the heroes had the best accommodations in another area.

When it was Noki's turn, and after the warm-up on Limpy's hand pads, he just stood up and got himself ready. This time his t-shirt was of Walt Disney's Seven Dwarfs.

"Once again, the irony notwithstanding, we need better shirts for you Noki", Bug said. Noki just shrugged his shoulders not understanding the joke that Bug himself could have been that cartoon on his shirt.

After the announcements and celebratory dancing around and cocky display by Broussard, the fight was on. The Ragin' Cajun tried to pounce on Noki quickly but Noki would have none of it. He was Oscar De La Hoya as he blocked every punch that came close. At other times, he was just out of range of Broussard's haymakers. It seemed his opponent was convinced that Noki had a glass chin and one punch would put him down. How else, they thought, would he have been knocked out so easily before?

By round three, Noki had made mincemeat of Broussard's left eye by making him eat jab after jab. The eye was swelling badly, and Broussard's frustration was starting to show. That's when Noki start to bang him to the body with vicious blows. With a few seconds left in the round, he dropped Broussard with a serious left uppercut to the solar plexus. Broussard was able to get a breather as the round was over. The crowd was worried, and they had good reason to be. The fight was about to be over.

When the fourth round came, Broussard charged hard, knowing he had to make things happen. Noki beautifully stayed out of range for everything and then at the right time threw an overhand right and left hook. Both connected. Broussard was out on his feet and slumped on the second rope. That was the only thing that kept him up as the referee intervened and ended the fight.

There was no celebration by Noki. That was not part of the thing he imitated from other fighters. He didn't understand it. He only copied what they did while actually boxing. He just walked back to his corner and nodded his head to Bug and Limpy, who were both jumping up in the air.

As per usual, the local crowd booed both Broussard and Noki. Bottles were thrown. Mayhem ensued and the group hastily got back to the losers locker room. They were the only one left as the other tomato cans had already received their money and gone home. And they waited.

"Here's your money. Now get the fuck out of here", is all the promoter said when he came in.

With more dents and bottles broken on their vehicle, the 2-7 Noki was now headed back home to Houston. Another long drive but another victory.

"He has two wins now and he looks great. No damage, either", Bug told Fay the next day.

"Is that true, Noki?" she asked.

"Yes, Ma'am", Noki replied.

They were at one of their monthly meetings with Fay to report in on their current situation. They felt good about telling her that they were financially doing a little better. They were at least paying their bills.

"It just doesn't feel right", Fay said, "I don't know why I am approving this. I mean is it right to use him? That even sounds bad. Noki, do you feel okay about this?"

"I like boxing," Noki said with a smile.

"I'm glad to hear that.," Fay replied as she turned to Bug. "I am torn about this. My job is definitely at stake. I am letting a man-child with severe autism put his life on the line. How can that be right?"

"I see your point", Bug replied, "We really don't have a choice. Besides, it's what he wants to do. And he is great at it."

"But what if he gets hurt? I don't know. There has to be a better way. There just has to be."

"We are all ears," Bug replied.

"I don't have any great ideas. And what about Jip? I heard there has been a lot more progress?" Fay inquired.

Noki's head fell to his chin as Bug replied, "He is sitting up. His right side is still weak but he is getting some movement We are hoping for a wheelchair soon but who knows? We go three times a week to visit him and watch boxing films with him. He seems to enjoy that."

"Great. And he knows about Noki?"

"No."

"Why not?"

"I'm afraid it will impede his recovery."

"Or are you afraid that he will say no?"

"That too."

"What did I say about being truthful?"

"Well, we haven't lied. And Noki's been brave."

"Well, at least you listened to my recommendations, but you have to tell Jip soon. Not telling him is basically a lie of omission and bad things happen when you lie".

"Okay, we will. I promise", Bug replied.

Chapter Twenty-Three

"Okay, we have slim pickings now", said Calzone.

"Which means?" asked Bug.

"Which means the word has gotten out. I think I can get him to fight Calvin Jackson in Austin because they are really a bunch of cocky rednecks there, but I have no idea after that."

"Is Jackson good?"

"Yup. He had a televised fight on a big undercard a few months back and looked great. He may even get ranked in the top twenty soon."

"So why will he fight a 2-7 fighter" asked Bug.

"His next televised fight is in 6 weeks on the undercard of Gideon's fight in Atlantic City. He needs a tune up to keep sharp."

"Does he know Noki can fight?"

"Not sure. He's good enough that they may not care. You would be in for a tough one here."

"The money?"

"You're getting greedy little man," Calzone laughed as he said it. "I can get you a couple grand for this one. But his people are pricks and it won't be friendly."

"We're used to that. You should see our car."

"Ha! Welcome to the boxing world. Now get the fuck out."

The Austin experience was different from the past few fights. Jackson's entourage was much bigger and more boisterous. They hovered around the morning weigh-ins. The gratuitous insults were again thrown at Noki, Bug and Limpy.

"Look at this fucking crew" said one of them, "They a bunch of cripples". They laughed at how Limpy walked and how small Bug was. "Your boy is going to get his mother-fucking ass chewed up tonight." Noki just stared at them and smiled.

"You a retard, boy?" another member asked.

"Leave him alone," said Limpy.

"Fuck you, beaner," he responded with the first of many slurs to Limpy's Mexican heritage.

After Jackson got off the scale Noki went to shake his hand and Jackson slapped it away. "Fuck outta here, you punk ass bitch. This ain't going to be no fight. I'm just going to get a sweat and then going to knock your shit out."

Noki just smiled and was not fazed at all. And he kept staring right through Jackson. And kept staring. After a few seconds of this awkward action, Jackson became uncomfortable. Never before had his intimidation tactics not had an effect.

"You hear me, bitch? Or are you deaf and dumb?"

Noki just kept smiling and staring and then Jackson shoved him hard in is chest. Noki regained his posture after being pushed about three feet back and almost hitting the floor. He continued to smile and walked right back to Jackson. Jackson's face had a confused look and then his henchman just pulled him to go leave and get breakfast.

Noki and his team had to watch a lot of film to figure out Jackson's weakness. He was good. Very good. What they did notice was that he kept his left hand down a lot. He kept it down after he threw a jab. He kept it down when he threw a hard right. It was Noki who really spotted this and felt that Juan Manuel Marquez would be his role model. Marquez was another incredible Mexican champ in his day and was known for his ability to catch fighters with his counter punching. If a fighter missed, he would pounce with big shots. That was Noki's plan.

After each fighter's entrance and introduction to the crowd, the pace of this fight was noticeably different from Noki's other matches as Jackson's skill was evident from the get-go. This time Noki took a few glancing shots from Jackson, more than any of his other fights. He was giving more openings to Jackson to lure in him. These were typical traps that Marquez would lay and for the first few rounds Noki had trouble landing a solid blow. The fight was scheduled for eight rounds and even though it was pretty much even, Bug and Limpy knew that they would not get a win without that knockout. But Jackson was getting comfortable and getting cocky. His jab was getting a little lazier after he threw it and was leaving himself exposed. That was what Noki was waiting on. In the fifth round it was evident that Jackson felt he was cruising and no longer worried. He was truly using this fight as a tune-up and boxing as if it was a sparring session. With a minute left to go in the round he threw one lazy jab too many as Noki timed it perfectly by stepping back and then throwing a powerful straight right hand counter punch to the left temple of Jackson's head. He never saw it and Jackson didn't wake up fully until he was in his locker room.

This time Noki, Bug and Limpy had no luck waiting for their money. No one came for them in the locker room. The lights were being turned off as they decided to go hunt down the promoter. They found him outside talking to his workers and about to get inside his car.

"Excuse me, sir. We didn't get paid."

The promoter reached inside his car and then got out after pulling out a baseball bat. Then two other men got out his car, one also with a bat and one with a tire iron.

"I'm sorry, I didn't hear you," the promoter said.

"There's no need for anyone to get hurt. Noki just needs to get paid. It's only fair", pleaded Bug.

"Fair? How about we bust your fucking skull and break your legs? That would be fair."

"I don't understand?" Bug asked.

"Understand? Explain to me how a 2-7 fighter is that good? Jackson doesn't lose to people like that. It was a set-up. Your boy is a ringer, so fuck off."

"It was a fair fight and Noki won. We need that money?"

"What you need is a lesson. Say another word and I'll give you one."

"But...." Bug tried to get out a sentence and that's when the promoter and his men started to quickly move towards the three of them. The only thing that stopped them in their tracks was the sound of three clicks of handguns.

"Pay him his money you hick fuck", said a heavily out of breath Frank Calzone, accompanied by the two men he played poker with regularly in his trailer.

"Calzone? That you? This is not your territory. We don't need to get messy here."

"The kid won. You were the ones getting messy. You're lucky I don't waste you right here."

"Sorry, Frankie. We were just playing around here. Here, here's your money", the promoter said as he paid Bug.

"Now take your piece of shit crew and get the fuck out of here", Frankie said.

"Okay. No hard feelings, Frankie, okay?"

"No. None at all. Should I tell Tommy about this?"

"No, please Frankie. It's all good. Here, take another five hundred," the promoter pulled more money from the wad he was holding. He then got in his car with the two other men and sped off.

"I told you this wasn't going to be easy", Frankie said to Bug.

"Did you see the fight?" Bug asked.

"No, I seen enough fights. I just don't like these hick fucks and thought we'd have some fun."

"You knew this would happen?" Bug asked.

"This fucking guy?" Frankie looked at his two other guys, "He thinks I'm a rookie".

"Well, thanks Frankie," Bug said. "Are all the fights and payments going to be like this?"

"Yes and no."

"What does that mean?" asked Bug.

"It means I can't pass this kid off as an easy loss to promoters anymore. And I'm not going to follow you around all the time. Got better things to do. You'll need a legit fight now and that's not my game."

"Why?"

"Do I seem legit to you?"

"Well…"

"There are certain people out there that think I am bad for boxing. Like I am some type of criminal. I don't know why they say such bad things about me. It's hurtful, really. All I try to do is help people".

"And we thank you for that."

"The truth is I can't legally be involved in promoting so all I can do is put your name out there. I know some people who put on real fights. Bigger venues. They may want your kid if something comes up. Don't know. You would need a break. These shit town, rowdy matches are not for you anymore."

"What's in it for you?" Bug asked.

"Are you questioning me? After all I did for you? You ungrateful little…."

"No. I'm sorry. I just don't understand."

"I'll let you in on a secret. I'm a gambler. That is how I make my money. I gamble on sure things. Your kid made me a lot of side money so far. I'm as disappointed as you that we can't play this game anymore. That being said, your boy, from what I heard, can fight. Maybe I'll throw a little money on him in Vegas or something if he gets some bigger matches. I don't know. Maybe if we put his face in the public's eye then casinos will lay odds on his fights. Who knows? I mean who the fuck is going to think a 3-7 could win any big fights? Could be easy money."

"Was that your plan all along?"

"I'm smart but I ain't that fucking smart. This kid can either really fight or has some pixie dust on him. Or both. Now go home. I got to find a diner to take a shit. All this gun-wielding does a number on my bowels."

"Thanks again, Frankie", Bug said as the three of them got in their car to drive home. It was a few hour trip through the night but now they had some good money to hold off the creditors. And hopefully hold off John and Gideon, who still wanted Carlo's Gym, as well.

CHAPTER TWENTY-FOUR

It was going to be a rough day. Bug convinced Noki that he had errands to do but instead went to see Jip. The facility was not the worst, but it was nowhere anyone would choose to live. Jip's recovery had finally taken a turn for the better over the past few weeks. He could transfer himself into the wheelchair from the bed. He could feed himself. And he could now talk with more clarity.

Bug found Jip watching the television. The volume was loud at first but Jip was able to find the remote and lower it.

"Where's Noki?"

"He's not here," Bug said.

"What's wrong? Is he ok?" Jip asked. Bug had never visited Jip alone before.

"Everything's fine. He's well. He's doing some stuff around the gym. I just came to talk to you about things."

"What things?" Jip responded coldly.

"Jip, you must know that the gym was not doing well."

"Yes, I'm sorry. I screwed up. I put all my eggs in one basket and that basket got taken away from me."

"So, you know about Gideon?"

"Yes".

"How?"

"John told me the night before my stroke. I blew it. But I am going to fix things."

"What does that mean?"

"It means I'm going to sell the whole thing so that Noki has something to live on", he responded sternly. It was at this point that Bug looked over and saw paperwork on the nightstand next to the hospital bed. He got up to go read it and saw that it was a letter of agreement to sell the gym and house to John.

"He was here?"

"Yes and he says this is our only option."

"When was he here?"

"About three days ago. Maybe four. Not sure."

"What else do you know?"

"I know what he told me and he told me that you are making Noki fight to keep the place going! What did I tell you about that, you traitor?"

"Hold on, hold on. That's not fair. And why are you listening to John?"

"He may be a snake but he is the only one telling me anything!"

"You were recovering. We were waiting until the right time. Please, don't sell anything yet."

"I have no choice. I know you need the money."

"We are doing okay, actually. Limpy is starting to get more white-collar fighters to pretend they are real boxers."

"That bullshit plan again? How many?"

"Four. It's a start".

"Won't work. And how could Noki have seven losses all by knockout? What have you done to my son?"

"Did John not tell you why he lost?"

"No, he just said that the commission is going to stop this charade soon. And in order for me to save Noki I have to sell the gym to him and that prick, Gideon."

"Well, he said that to me too. And you are the only one who can sell it. But if you do it won't make enough money to keep Noki financially free but for a few years. Then what?"

"I don't know. Maybe I will start another gym or something. It's not your worry. Anyway, explain to me how Noki could lose?"

"Because he wanted to. Because we knew you didn't want any chance of him getting hurt. It was his plan to not win."

"He faked his knockouts?"

"Yes."

Jip started to smile. It was crooked but it was definitely a smile. "The Mouse", he said.

"Yes, he copied Bruce 'The Mouse' Strauss".

"How did you get the fights? Wait, don't tell me. Calzone?"

"Yes."

"How did he look before getting knocked out?"

"He was better than all of them by a longshot, Jip. The kid can fight. "

Jip was actually beaming with pride. "I know he can. But now he is just a loser to everyone. Just like me."

"Not exactly."

"What do you mean?"

"Well, we had no option but to try winning. Calzone got us a fight with that Mendez kid in San Antonio".

"And?"

"Knocked him out. Then he fought the Ragin' Cajun."

"And?"

"Knocked him out."

"Any others?"

"Yup."

"Who?"

"Calvin Jackson."

Jip cringed. He was afraid to ask but he did. "And?"

"Knocked him out."

"Unbelievable. Who did he fight as?"

"Joe Louis, De La Hoya and Marquez. In that order."

"Brilliant. He's amazing, isn't he? He can be any fighter and almost be as good as that fighter. Maybe as good."

"Yes. But this is why I am here. I need your thoughts. I need you involved. Noki needs to know you approve."

"I can't. I promised my wife....."

"Those days are gone Jip. We have no choice now. We need the money."

Jip sat quiet. He was running the scenarios through his mind. And then it hit him. "Wait, you have got to be stuck. These wins were not televised right?"

"Right?"

"So that means no one really cares about Noki. No one is connecting the dots that he may be good. It's the opposite. No one is going to fight him now because they don't want to be shown up by a 3-7 fighter."

"You're right, except we got a call yesterday."

"From?"

"They are having a televised event on ABC for the four Olympic champions from last summer's games. It's called *Night of Gold* and they want to showcase them to the public. "

"Jake Landry?"

"Yeah, they have had two fighters pull out on him. They are desperate. They can sell Noki because of his last three fights."

"Landry is fast and experienced. He must have had a hundred amateur fights."

"We have been watching fights. Noki has come up with two ideas. Archie Moore or…."

"Definitely, Archie Moore," Jip interrupted, "Wait, why am I agreeing on this? You went behind my back and now Noki could get hurt or get someone else really hurt."

"Jip, I came into your life months ago for some unknown reason. I came into Noki's life for some unknown reason. Then all hell broke loose. I'm only trying to help keep us all together and save us. You,

118

Noki, the cat, the fish, Limpy, me, and the people at the gym. Maybe that's why I am here. It doesn't matter. I haven't stolen anything from you. I haven't manipulated Noki. I never lied to you. That is why I am here."

"I can't do it. I'm signing those papers. He is all I have."

"But you'll lose him if you do that."

"At least no one gets hurt."

"Don't they? It seems to me someone will get hurt no matter what choice you make."

"I'm done talking. Go away."

"Jip, please. "

"Nurse.....nurse....get him out."

Bug took the hint and left.

When Bug returned to the gym, he found Noki getting ready to practice. Emotionless as always, Bug went up to him to tell him the news.

"Noki...."

"You told Papa, didn't you?"

Bug was taken aback. "How did you know?"

Noki just shrugged his shoulders. "He doesn't want you fighting. I'm sorry."

"I like boxing. I want to fight. So....(he stared at the wall for a few uncomfortable seconds)... I am going to fight."

"I'm not sure it's that easy, Noki"

"Why, I'm my own person. A real man now. I will show everyone."

"You don't have to prove anything, Noki."

Noki looked confused. "Prove?" he asked.

"We know you are a good fighter. Heck, a great fighter."

"I just want to fight. So, that's what I am going to do." Noki climbed into the ring to warm up by shadow boxing.

Bug was now frustrated. He had no idea what to do. He was stuck. Jip didn't want his son fighting but it may not matter anymore. He started to wonder whether Noki has the wherewithall to make that decision. Did his autism preclude him from making his own decisions? What was he trying to show people? He also knew that without him taking this fight the gym would go into a death spiral. It may not matter if Jip gives those papers back to John. It would be all over. He had to drive back and talk to Jip.

When he arrived at the nursing home, he ran different scenarios of things to say to Jip. None of them were good enough to work. He knew it was a lost cause since no one was compromising. That's when he saw a familiar sight as he knocked on the open door to Jip's room. The blue outfit gave it away. It was Fay.

"Hi, Bug", she said. It was clear that she had been there for a while.

"Why are you here?" Bug asked.

"Well, I am the social worker in charge of this case. I decided to come over here and talk with Jip a bit."

"And?"

"And she is just as big a pain in the ass as you!" Jip interrupted.

"Now Jip, you don't mean that. Stop being such a curmudgeon. Tell him what we talked about", Fay said.

"This lady is pretty smart and has a great heart. She talked me through things after you left."

"What does that mean?" asked Bug.

"It means you are all in a pickle," responded Fay. "I don't like any of this but financially you are trapped. Selling the gym is an option but I don't think it may be enough with Jip's recovery bills".

"I'm confused," said Bug.

"If Jip gets released then he needs somewhere to go. The doctors have told me that could be a few weeks or a month at best. His house has to be equipped to handle him and so do you all."

"We can make it work".

"Maybe you can, maybe you can't. Medicare will pay for much of the stuff needed for him to live there. They love getting people back home. That's where it will stop. If you sell and get a small place you all will still run out of money eventually. Either way you need a source of income."

"The gym will come around eventually. I just know it", replied Bug.

"Yeah, but when? "

"Eventually Limpy will get more regular Joes in there. They pay monthly, too. It could work in time. Until then, well, Noki is really our only hope."

"Yes, I know that, but we have a lot of questions about that. I have contacted by DHS and they are now doing an investigation. Jip also doesn't want him used as a pawn."

"But he's not a pawn. This has been his plan as much as anyone else's".

"That's the dilemma. Can he convince others of that? If there is a hearing, can he prove that he is capable of making that decision?" asked Fay.

"He's not mentally disabled. He is autistic but it is still his choice. Trust me, I would be the first person to stop him from being used", said Bug.

"Bullshit. You made him your puppet! You and Calzone!" screamed Jip.

"Now, Jip, you need to stop," Fay responded, "I have been with these two since this whole thing started. I told you that. It has been pretty brave what they have been doing and they have followed your wishes as best as they could. "

"I'm not happy about this. I have let my wife down. I have let Noki down. I have ruined it all."

"Not true. You did your best. Now let Noki help you. It seems that is really what he wants to do. Isn't that correct, Bug?" said Fay.

"Kind of", Bug said.

"What does that mean?" asked Fay.

"I'm not really sure. I mean he does want to help, don't get me wrong. He has a heart of gold. And he really wants to fight. He likes it. There just seems to be something else in it for him."

"Because he feels important or special?" Fay asked.

"I don't know, he says he is a real man now. Maybe he thinks he is meant to do this. Like it's his purpose in life."

"I guess the real question is where do we go from here? What is your plan , Bug?" Fay queried.

"I say let him fight because…." Bug started to say.

"No, this Landry kid is great. There is no way they will give him the win", Jip interjected.

"Hold on, Jip," Fay said, "Let him finish."

"Listen, I don't understand much about this boxing game. It is crooked as anything I have lived through before and I thought I saw the worst. No one seems to make real money unless they get large televised fights. No one gets those fights unless they have a spotless record with about twenty wins and then they break into that upper echelon. It's all political, too, because you need the right manager, promoter and connections for that. Noki has none of that. Somehow, however, by losing he won. Now that he has gotten past some very good fighters, he is getting those big fights because they think he is an easy win. It's bizarre, to say the least. For whatever reason, he is now in a position to make money if he wins this fight against Landry. With this win and the Jackson win before, I am told that could move up quickly even though he has a bad record. Has that ever happened before, Jip?"

"Freddie Pendleton."

"Who?"

"He was a guy that was 7-7-1 and everyone thought he was a nobody. He turned his career around and even ended up lightweight champ. He fought everyone. Tough as nails."

"So, there is a precedent."

"Yes," said Jip, "But it's a different time now."

"Which means?" asked Bug.

"Which means he can't lose again. He has to win this fight and they won't give him a decision. He has to knock Landry out."

"That's the plan," replied Bug.

"What are you saying, Jip?" asked Fay.

"One fight. That's it. And I'm coming. You can't stop me. That's my son. If he starts getting hurt, I will throw in the towel. You hear me?"

"But the fight is next week. In Vegas."

"I'm coming. Get me the hell out of here."

"You have to convince the doctors," said Fay.

"My ass. I can get in and out of my wheelchair. I can piss in a toilet with a little help. I'm coming. It's the only way I'll let this fight happen."

Bug laughed but also knew it was the only way. "Well, I guess we have to do what we have to do."

Chapter Twenty-Five

TV ANNOUNCERS:

"We are on to the main event and I am not even sure how this fight was approved," said Teddy Atlas.

"Now, Teddy, let's not go there. It's been a great night for our gold medalists as they are finally getting some limelight. The crowd has been great, and they want to see these guys. You can hear them chant "USA, USA, USA".

"I'm all for America, Joe, but this is quite ridiculous. Landry, our best American fighter in the games, is already 8-0 and this kid, Polendina, has been knocked out seven times".

"Yes, I know that, but he got a couple of nice wins lately."

"I get that. But seven knockouts? He must have a glass chin."

"I guess we'll see because he is coming towards the ring now. Is that a dwarf with him?" questioned Joe.

"Is this some sort of joke," Atlas asked.

"I don't think so."

"The other guys with him? What is that? One is limping badly, and one is in a wheelchair. Even his team is disabled. And the kid doesn't even have a robe. He's even wearing a Peter Pan shirt", said Atlas.

"It is interesting. Ok, let's see how this goes. They're in the ring now and here comes Landry. The fans are starting to chant again."

The stare down, after their names and records were announced, was typical. Noki just stared as Landry had a cocky grin shaking his head up and down as the ref gave directions.

Noki walked to his corner and looked at Jip who said, "Stay with the plan and tend to business".

"Well, here we go. Let's see what this kid can do," Joe said to Teddy.

As the bell rang Noki became Archie Moore. It was a very distinct style not seen in in a very long time. Landry began throwing punches but Noki was blocking them.

"Teddy, what is Polendina doing in there?"

"That's the 'lock'!"

"The 'lock'?" Joe asked.

"This kid is fighting like the Old Mongoose, Archie Moore. And, you know what, Joe, he does it really well."

"Did you know he fights like that?"

"I know nothing about this kid. There were some clips on him from the Jackson fight, but he fought nuthin' like this."

Noki kept coming forward and blocking punches. The first round was a loss as Landry threw a ton of shots, but most were blocked. Noki's punches were mainly left hooks to the body and they had some effect. Round two was similar. This time Noki pressed forward with a few stiff jabs that hurt Landry while still catching him with body blows.

"Explain this lock to me, Teddy?" Joe asked

"It's called the 'cross armed guard'. It stops the straight punches that Landry is known for. He was a great amateur, but those guys tend to throw those punches in a direct line and the lock only exposes only the top of the head of the guy doing it. Makes them really hard to hit. It is thoroughly confusing Landry."

"What's he looking to do with it?"

"Well, he covers himself up like a turtle. The thing is he better have a power shot, a big left hook, for it to work and that has to be coming…."

"He's down! Landry is down! Polendina caught him with a massive left hook here in round two", said Joe.

"I can't believe it. The kid is going to win this fight. I can't believe it. It's Archie Moore reincarnated," said Teddy.

"The ref has stopped the fight as Landry is out cold. What an upset. Teddy, your thoughts?"

"I'm flabbergasted. It was a beautiful style. And like I always say, styles make fights."

Jip stayed in his wheelchair as Limpy and Bug jumped around the ring in excitement. Everyone was stunned: the fans, the announcers and the other corner. Everyone but Noki, who was emotionless. After the decision was given by the ring announcer, Teddy Atlas took to the ring to talk to Noki on live television. This took everyone by surprise. Bug and Limpy didn't prepare for this part.

"Tyrone, where did learn to fight like that?" asked Teddy.

"Noki", Noki responded.

"Excuse me?"

Noki pointed to himself and said it again, "Noki."

"I'm confused," said Teddy as looked down at Bug and then to Limpy.

"His name is Noki", said Bug.

"Okay, ummm Noki, I see that you fought like Archie Moore tonight. I have seen a clip of you before, but you fought differently. How long did you work on getting that style down?"

"I just pretend."

"Okay. Ummm," Teddy stammered as he was confused, "What were you thinking in there as he was throwing all those punches? You didn't seem bothered by it. He's a great fighter. A gold medalist."

"I have fun boxing."

The short sentences were perplexing Teddy. Noki didn't respond like other fighters who would thank God, their team or their mother and then give long-winded answers that made for good television interviews.

"Okay, this was a major upset. What's next for you?" Teddy asked.

"I am going to save us because I am good at boxing".

"Yes, ummm, ok. But with this win and the Jackson win you may get a shot at another contender. And now the world has seen your cross-guard style. So other fighters will be prepared for you. Are you ready for that? "

Noki had no answer. He just stared. After a long silence Bug spoke up and said, "He prepares harder than anyone. All Noki is looking for is a shot at bigger fights and bigger paydays".

"I have to go now", Noki interrupted, "I need to take care of Papa". And with that he ended the interview by walking away. Bug and Limpy followed as they climbed out of the ring to get Jip and roll away. Teddy looked back at the camera with a totally befuddled face. "Okay, Joe, back to you."

After the commercial Teddy and Joe closed the show with their synopsis.

"An interesting night, Teddy, what do you think?" Joe asked.

"I'm stunned. I'm confused. The first three guys did really well. They proved why they were gold medalists. Landy took a big loss here and has to regroup now. He fought his usual style and was confused by a smarter fighter."

"Smarter?"

"Yes, smarter. It was the perfect style to beat a straight up boxer with much of Landry's amateur technique still dominating how he fights."

"And Polendina? I mean he has a record of 4-7 but four straight wins all by knock out. Can that continue?"

"Well, he is a different cat. Doesn't say much. Quirky. Just does his job and goes to work. I want to see more of him. And that crew that works with him. I need to see more of them too. I remember his dad now, Jip Polendina. He was a decent fighter and trainer in his day. There's a legacy there but I'm not sure of the relation to Jip. Not even sure where Noki came from. I love it. Just one name. Like Cher or Bono. Cracks me up. But the kid has power and can hit. I hope to see him again."

CHAPTER TWENTY-SIX

Noki and the team made their way home. Jip went back to the rehab facility but the plan was now to set the house up for him. Bug was able to work with Fay to get the right people to make some ramps and do other things to accommodate Jip and make it wheelchair accessible. The good news was that Jip was starting to use a walker and not many changes were needed to just some handrails for the bathroom and such.

The world had heard of Noki now. Locally, in Houston, the press wanted to get the scoop but Bug and Limpy decided they needed some cover. They really felt Noki was not prepared to do interviews. They also didn't want to let his autism be a distraction. No one knew how that would go. They were able to do this for the first week as reporters were directed only to Bug. They made Noki "unavailable". The first story in the Houston Chronicle highlighted Noki's improbable win. "Loser Turned Winner" was the headline and the gist of piece. The positive part of the whole thing was more white-collar fighters were now interested in Carlo's Gym. Limpy was training 8 to 10 people each night and their monthly fees started to offset some expenses. Everything was going great until a follow up story came out a week later. Noki was exposed.

The phone kept ringing on the Monday morning after their regular run. Everyone wanted to know more about the fighter with a mental disability. Bug was confused until he retrieved a newspaper and read the story. There were only two others who really could have talked. Calzone was one of them, but no one knew about him. He was a shadow figure and would never talk to the press. He would never put himself in that position. The other person was the obvious culprit. John knew enough about Noki and wanted to sink the whole ship and the anonymous quotes were obviously his. "This kid's strings are being pulled. It's abuse, I tell ya." And then, "The whole bunch of them are con artists over there. I think he lost all of his fights on purpose. They scammed people. Oh, he can fight, but they let him get knocked out. If he meant to do it then they all should be put in jail. If he didn't then how could anyone let a retarded person go in there and get hurt? It needs to be stopped."

The next phone call that Bug picked up made his heart drop. It was Fay.

"We have a problem, Bug", Fay said.

"What's that?"

"I already got the call from someone at Human Services. They have a record of Noki. They know his issues. They are calling for an investigation. "

"What do we do?"

"Well, I'm not sure. My job is at stake too. But we are in this together. "

The next few weeks were a blur, one that Noki never noticed. He still ran in the morning with the fighters and trained during the 3:00 pm session. He was told about everything and certainly understood the severity of it. He just didn't seem to care and shrugged it off.

There were crowds now and Limpy had to set up chairs and rope off areas. This was new to all of them. That was the fun part. The gym was getting great exposure. Everyone wanted to see the autistic savant who was knocking people out. They also received many phone calls for upcoming fights. Bug ran everything by Jip who was about to come home in the next few days. The offers were worth good money, especially being on the undercard of a title fight on HBO. That title fight was Gideon's first defense of his belt. It was awkward but something that they didn't want to turn down. If Noki could beat Sebastian Dupree, who was ranked third in the world, he was sure to get the winner of the Gideon vs. Smith fight. They had a month to prepare. Unfortunately, none of it mattered. The Texas Boxing Commission suspended Noki's license until they could finish their own investigation. They, too, were tipped off, probably by John, but stated that their decision would be dependent on the outcome of the DHS case. Noki's fight in Las Vegas was now put on hold as that state commission concurred and agreed with the Texas Boxing Commission. Things were about to get messy.

The day Jip got home was great for Noki. He was as happy as anyone had ever seen him. Bug gladly offered to give his office back, but Jip would have none of it. He wanted Bug to continue to manage Carlo's Gym because of how well he, and Limpy, had done. He knew those days were over for him. He would continue to consult with them about Noki's career, if it was to continue.

"So, this is the famous Carlo's Gym?" asked Fay.

"You heard of it?" asked Bug.

"No, just what I read in the paper. I just came by to see how Jip was doing. Is everything okay?"

"Yeah, we got him all set. Why are you not at the office today?"

"I am on paid leave. They suspended me until they figure this mess out."

"I'm so sorry, Fay."

"Not your fault. I feel good about what we did. I actually saw Noki's fight. He's incredible. Why should he not be allowed to continue?"

"I guess you missed out on what all the haters are saying? We have had protesters outside every day. There are a lot of angry people out there who feel we took advantage of him. My stomach is in knots. Maybe we did?"

"We did not but that's what the investigation and court case will be about."

"It started already?" Bug asked.

"Yes, DHS is talking to everyone. From what I am hearing, they are talking to every promoter and fighter he fought. They are on the line for this, too. They don't want to look bad. To clear him, there has to be overwhelming evidence that he has the capacity to make his own decision to fight."

Over the next week Bug was interviewed multiple times by people representing the state. So was Jip and even Limpy. The only one not questioned was Noki, but that time was coming. Bug felt unprotected because they had no representation. That is until one of the white-collar boxers, a lawyer, offered to help them in their case pro bono. Steven Barker was a pretty well-known defense attorney around town. He was a middle age man who found joy again in his workouts at Carlo's.

"I got this, guys", Steven said, "No one talks anymore to anyone without me. I will have my own team work on their own investigation. Let's meet after closing and all of us can talk."

The whole team was at the meeting: Noki, Jip, Limpy, Bug and even Fay. They fessed up to everything. No detail was left out, not even Calzone. Barker was impressed but was visibly worried.

"Well, shit, we have work to do. This won't be simple. DHS has to cover their ass and don't want to be responsible for Noki getting hurt. I understand their perspective."

"And the boxing commission?'

"They don't give a crap. I have been involved with them before. They'll defer to the DHS case. Don't worry about them."

"But we need this next fight to keep the gym going. How long until the case comes up?"

"I am going to have to do some politicking here, guys. I will need to use the press in our favor to move it up sooner. I need to push back and say they are denying his right to make a living and this needs to be settled soon. I'm on it. Just have Noki keep training."

The next week a third story come out about Noki, this time concentrating on the case. No longer was Bug or anyone at the gym interviewed. They were closed off from giving any more information, per Barker's wishes. The article was more in Noki's favor this time. It highlighted his skill and his major wins. It detailed the need for him to keep fighting in order to keep the gym afloat; especially now that Jip was in need of help as well. It came off as a heart-breaking story that made the DHS a bad guy for limiting their chances of survival. It also pressured the state to move the case up to two weeks prior to the fight. Bug was able to get the promoter of the Las Vegas fight to keep him on the card with the caveat that they would have another fighter ready to take his place if things went south. And that was a big "if". Bug knew the only reason they would do this was due to the ratings Noki would give them. The press, and the attention that came with it, made Noki a big ticket item now. He was an anomaly. The "fighting savant" is what they called him and this meant fans wanted to see him and watch thefight.

"Whatever happens, I want you to know that I appreciate all that you have done, Jip said to Bug one late evening after they all ate supper. Noki had gone to his room to watch films.

"Thank you", replied Bug.

"I know you always had Noki's best interest in mind. And mine as well. I failed us but you have made this thing work. You and Noki. Even Limpy with his white-collar boxing thing. Anyway, I love Noki. I was just trying to keep him from all this. I wanted him safe. But you guys actually saved me."

"Not true. Noki saved us. And I'm not sure he is a boy anymore, Jip. Especially not in the ring."

"I told you. He can fight."

"You did. But I want to thank you for giving me a chance. I was a wanderer. A nobody. All I cared about was myself. You gave me the opportunity to be here and care about others like you and especially Noki. I was destined to be here for some reason", Bug said.

"Like a bolt out of the blue, fate steps in and sees you through."

"That's nice. Did you just make that up?" asked Bug

"No, it's a song from one of Noki's movies he used to watch as a kid all the time. Don't remember the name. He used to sing over and over."

CHAPTER TWENTY-SEVEN

The medical assessment was key to Noki's case. Barker and the DHS agreed on a local physician who they were confident would give an impartial opinion. That visit was four days prior to the case being presented to the three members of the Department of Human Services. The only ones invited to the hearing were Noki, Bug, Jip, Limpy and their lawyer Steven Barker. Outside the building was a whole other matter. The media had created a monster with this case. Many of the protesters were carrying signs that said, "Slavery, no more" or "Using disabled people for personal gain is a crime!". Their chants and echoes could be heard inside the hearing room. This worried Barker and he knew that the tribunal of DHS members may bend to this pressure.

Noki was asked to sit at a table opposite the tribunal members with Barker at his side. Behind them sat the rest of the crew. This was not a trial but it felt like one. The investigation was done but DHS wanted to ask some final questions before they made a decision.

Before they started, all of them took an oath to tell the truth, similar to what you would see in a court of law. Then the main person, the local DHS commissioner, spoke:

"Okay, let's get this started. Tyrone Polendina?."

There was no response from Noki.

"Tyrone?"

"Sir, he goes by the name of Noki," said Steven Barker

"Why?"

"I don't even know".

"Okay, no matter. Ty....er....Noki, good morning."

Noki just smiled.

"Can he talk?"

"Yes, sir, he can talk," said Steve.

"I'm sorry. I guess I meant, will he talk?"

"He may. He may not."

"Ok, no matter. Noki. We have thoroughly reviewed this case. In particular, we have examined the facts both that were presented to us and those we found when we sent our investigators to uncover information. There is much attention to this case, and we understand the importance of it, to both you but to others to come. We want to summarize what we know and then have you add some more so we may make a proper decision. Does that sound okay?"

Noki just smiled. "Yes, sir", replied Steven for Noki.

"Well, here we go. We know that you were given a diagnosis of autism at a young age. This was after you were adopted by one Jip Polendina and his wife. And that is Jip behind you, correct?"

"It is, sir", said Barker.

"Okay, you did receive a home school education and did pass a GED, so you have a high school diploma. During the past year, after your father had his stroke, you have been boxing as a professional. Your first seven fights were losses via knockout. Somehow that slipped everyone's attention. Is this correct?"

"Yes, sir", said Barker.

"Now there was some controversy over whether you truly tried to win those fights or not. This is beyond the scope of this hearing. In fact, every promoter and boxer involved in those fights refused to talk with us. There was mention of some involvement with a Frank Calzone, an unsavory character with a long history with the legal system. Unfortunately, he was nowhere to be found to even interview".

Bug smiled when he heard this. He loved the word unsavory to describe Calzone. Nothing could be more unsavory than him. Even so, Calzone, in a weird way, could be trusted especially when it was in his favor to do so.

"So, we could only go on the official record", continued the DHS state commissioner. "This mess would have probably been easy to decide, and stop, if it was brought to our attention earlier. Unfortunately, no one tipped us off that this was a concern until you went ahead and won four straight fights over what we were told were impressive combatants. Is that correct?"

Noki shook his head yes but was staring away at a single point in the distance. Though he looked like he was not paying attention, he often was.

"All by knockout? "

Noki shook his head again but this time with a smile.

"Congratulations. It is obvious that you can fight. The question is whether you are competent to understand the consequences of your actions, which means the risk that goes along with boxing such as brain injury or even death. So, the question is, Noki, do you understand that you can die if you box?"

Noki smiled but did not answer.

"I do need an answer here, son", repeated the commissioner.

"Noki, please answer", said Barker, which was then repeated by Bug.

"I am not going to die. I win. And I save everyone else."

"That wasn't the question", said the DHS commissioner, "Do you know that you could get hurt and even die in the ring?"

Silence. Noki was thinking. Then he spoke up again and said, "I am not going to die or get hurt. I save everyone. That's what happens."

"Okay, so this again is our issue", said the DHS commissioner, "We cannot tell if he understands the consequences of his actions. Let me bring in the doctor who examined him".

Dr. Roy Walt was brought in after waiting out in the hallway. A middle-aged man with a paunch, he seemed to have a distressed expression on his face that went along with a disheveled look, even though he had a white jacket and tie on.

"Dr. Walt, what are your conclusions on this case?"

"All I was asked was to determine in this case is Noki's competency. It is obvious that Noki has pretty severe autism. His mannerisms and eye contact and inability to pick up social cues make me believe that is the correct diagnosis. I know that he has a GED from high school. I also have been told that he can do the normal activities of daily living. He can clean for himself, cook for himself, drive an automobile and such. Unfortunately, he did not answer many questions for me, which makes this case so very hard. My issue is not whether he is competent on how to take care of himself. He is. My issue, which I told to DHS, is whether he understands the consequences of being a boxer, that being brain injury and death. And I still don't know."

"Thank you, Dr. Walt", said the DHS commissioner, "From what I did not hear today from Noki and from what I did hear from the doctor and our investigators prior, I think I am leaning towards stopping this from travesty before it gets worse".

"May we speak?" asked Barker.

"Yes", said the DHS commissioner.

"Noki, has been around boxing his whole life. He has seen the good and the bad. He knows the consequences more than you do, and I mean no disrespect by that."

"I don't understand?" said one of the DHS members in the tribunal.

"Well, he has sparred before. He has fought 12 professional fights. He has been hit and hurt before. Don't you think that anyone who is getting hit knows the consequence of those punches; that being pain and damage?"

"Even with his severe autism?"

"Does an animal put its limb in a fire and keep it there? Does a deer know to stay away from certain areas that are unsafe? It is nature itself that teaches life to stay out of harm's way. Noki has to fight against this urge to put himself in harm's way in order to pursue his career."

The three started to talk and as the head commissioner held his hand over the mic so that their conversation was neither heard nor recorded. This lasted a minute or so.

"I think that point is interesting but not enough to sway us", said the commissioner.

"Okay, let me change my argument a bit. Of all the boxers you have interviewed, how many understand the consequences of their career choice? Brain damage and death?"

"We haven't interviewed any other boxers".

"What? So how is it fair to ask Noki these questions? You don't have a baseline to compare it too."

The members of the tribunal started whispering to each other again. Barker continued.

"Listen, I don't want to go all 'legal' on you here. This is not a courtroom and Noki is not on trial. Or is he? Anyway, it sure seems you are ready to hand out a life sentence."

"No, this is not a trial and that is not true", said the commissioner.

"Isn't it? Listen, if you feel Noki has the ability to be competent in other aspects of his life ,then you need to believe he is as competent to make his own career choice. I really don't want to bring up the Americans with Disability Act because that is where this will go. We have a potential employer, a boxing promoter, who wants to employ Noki and you are stopping his ability to earn a living."

The three in the tribunal started to talk to each other again....

"Lady and gentlemen, you are getting caught up in areas you know nothing about. Your heart is in a good place. Noki appreciates that. As a father of a son with Down's Syndrome, I appreciate that.

This is a sticky situation and if Noki was unable to protect himself then I could see your point. But this is different. The issue is his competency. The doctor states he is competent in all other areas of his life, and you must protect Noki's constitutional right and preserve the moral dignity of this process. Forget the protests. Forget the media. Those are irrelevant."

"Aare they? I am not so sure about that?" said the only woman on the tribunal.

"What do you mean?" asked Barker.

"Well, our investigators found this Bug character to have lived a life that was very unsavory as well".

Bug was less amused at that word now. He gulped and then slumped in his chair.

"He was known to work in carnivals, in strip clubs and in slimy professional wrestling gigs all around the country. Now you have him peddling Noki around to the highest bidder. I see Noki's father is now involved but you can see how this looks?"

"No, I do not?"

"Well, you have a white man using a black, excuse me, African-American man to make him money."

"That's a lie!" screamed Jip.

"This is all untrue," Barker interrupted as he gave Jip a look, "It may look like that to some, but many people can see the same image and get two different pictures or perspectives. What you are saying is only one viewpoint, a negative and an untrue one. Our viewpoint is that....."

"I want to box! I know what punches can do. I'm not stupid", Noki blurted out.

"What?" said the commissioner.

"I want to box! My choice.", Noki said as he stared this time at the tribunal.

"And that is the other viewpoint", said Barker.

After an hour of deliberation, the group got the news they needed and left the meeting only to be met at the steps of the front door by the press and by protesters.

"Shame on you!" screamed one protestor.

"Slavery no more!" yelled another.

"No more human cockfighting!" said another.

Steven Barker stood at the podium in front of the microphones and repeated what everyone had heard. Noki was going to be allowed to fight. It seemed like most of the crowd was very angry and started to boo.

Barker continued, "I understand your concerns. Really, I do and more than you know. We don't want anyone, anywhere, to be used for another's gain."

Noki, Bug, Jip and Limpy stood by silent. Noki was staring into the distance.

"We need not let others dictate our feelings, however. Please have an open mind. I see your perspective and so did the DHS board. But please understand that Noki is a great fighter and wasn't being thrown in to get beat up. His first fights notwithstanding, he has beaten great boxers and deserves a chance to earn a living. That is the law. It's also what he wants to do, and he has openly said that today and he understands the consequences of doing so. That is why this decision was made in our favor."

The crowd would have none of it. They started to hiss and boo again. And then the chants started. Barker was about to leave when he spoke again.

"I have one more person that wants to talk to you. My son."

Colin Barker was a man in his early 20s with Down's Syndrome. He was a smallish figure with the typical features of the syndrome. The crowd stopped and there was complete silence as he took to the mic.

"I am proud of my dad for what he has done. I am proud of Noki. Why can't we be happy for someone with special needs who is finally doing what he wants?" he said and took pause. There was no more shouting.

"I have been in the Special Olympics my whole life. I wish you were there to cheer for us. How many of you have ever been?"

More silence.

"Now we Special Olympians have someone to cheer for and you're mad? That's not fair. Noki is my hero, whether he wins or loses. And you can't stop that."

You could hear a pin drop as Colin went over to hug Noki. It was a clash of two different disabilities. Colin hugged him hard, very typical of highly emotional and loving person with Down's Syndrome. Noki, without expression, with his autism, didn't understand how to hug like this and barely reciprocated. The protest was over. All of them left as they cut through the crowd. There was a mixture of mumbling and tears and confusion.

As Noki got into the car to go, Barker went over Bug, Jip and Limpy, and said, "He needs to win now. If he gets hurt then I'll be done. I put my career on the line here and even got my son got involved. Please don't let us down."

"He never has", Jip said.

"And one more thing. Luckily, they didn't dig too much into your finances but I need a guy in my firm to come over there and help you out. From what my team found, you guys are a mess".

The drive home was a quiet one, especially after all the noise during the protests. No one really wanted to speak much. Everyone was happy but they also knew what was at stake. Noki had to fight in two weeks against the number three ranked fighter in the world. And he had to win. This fight was for $20,000, which was massive for the team, but that money would still go quickly towards Jip's expenses and medical bills, which were already piling up.

That night Bug laid in his cot trying to fall asleep, but his mind wouldn't let him. He was nervous and his thoughts were scattered. He was bothered by the term "unsavory" and how they used it for both he and Frank Calzone. He also didn't like the accusations about using Noki but he knew now that it was partly true. He wasn't the one fighting. He wasn't a real trainer. Though his intentions were pure he still needed Noki to lead the way. At least he took the lead role in helping. He could have run away, like he always did before, when things got rough but for some reason he didn't. He needed meaning in his life and maybe helping Noki was it, he thought. Being accused of putting Noki in harm's way definitely didn't sit well, however. His ego was bruised, and he wished he didn't even have an ego. As he tried to tease all this out, he started to think about how Noki handled things. With his autism, it looks like he is not focused or overly focused. It looks like he may be hard of hearing. Maybe there was more to Noki? Maybe he is egoless? Maybe he understands everything and just let's things go? It's obvious that Noki has social issues but maybe there was more to the story? Bug's mind wouldn't stop. He wondered whether Noki's autism gave him the ability to not let things bother him. Without an ego he never worries about the past or future but only the moment. It's as if Noki has the mental clarity or the gift of having no thought at all? This means no stress, no worry and just being.....Noki. At that moment, Bug realized how great this kid was. And he was jealous.

CHAPTER TWENTY-EIGHT

The next day was absolute chaos. It started early after the morning run. Steven Barker's coworker, Bob, came in to "help". He was given full access to the office by Jip and that is where he sat. Phone calls kept ringing while he worked and Jip and Bug both answered the calls and as well as questions by Bob. The press wanted to know about Noki and his autism. Bob wanted to know about bank accounts, wills, power-of-attorney and more.

"You guys are a goddamn mess", said Bob, "How the hell have you functioned so far? I called over to get an accountant here this afternoon. What we are going to do is get your will done Jip. We need you to name a medical and financial power of attorney. Will that be Bug?"

"Yes".

"Bug, I need your real name."

"Jim Grillo".

"Do you have a driver's license?"

"I do not".

"Do you drive?"

"Sometimes".

"Oh my god. Give me what you have. "

Bug passed him his whole wallet. They continued their conversation for quite a while. They made a plan to set up individual bank accounts for each person; Jip, Noki and Bug. They then discussed at length how people were to be paid from Noki's fights. Noki would get 70% of earnings and Jip, Limpy and Bug would each get 10%. This was to be after expenses were paid. Bob stayed until the accountant showed up later and they worked on a plan to save money and spend money, etc. In other words, a budget. This was a major change for the crew, but one needed to make sure they were well taken care of as well pass the smell test when others would try to snoop on them looking for improprieties. Now all they had to do was make some money. And that was starting to happen.

Limpy's idea of making the gym more accommodating to the layperson really was catching on, especially after the press for Noki. They were now up to 20 people paying monthly and this was starting to grow. After discussing this with Bob and the accountant, they decided to bring Limpy in for a full-time position to run classes throughout the day when the time comes. The morning would have training sessions for white-collar men and women, and this would continue throughout the day until the real fighters came in at 3 PM and trained until 5PM and then another session with white-collar boxers. They now needed to market this plan, which came a little more easily now that people were coming in just to see Noki. There were fans of all types who just wanted a glimpse of the boxing anomaly. Word was spreading about Carlo's Gym; proving that they just may have a chance to make it. The only thing that broke up all the good news was the phone call from the promoter in Vegas. Noki no longer had an opponent. He supposedly injured his hand. The other possibility was that he didn't want to fight Noki. No one knew for sure. The promoter needed two things from Bug and Noki. He needed them to sign the papers to be under contract and they needed him to agree to fight a smaller sized heavyweight. These two issues weren't easily remedied because the contract was now in Bob's hands.

Promoters usually exclusively sign fighters to a multi-fight deal or else they won't put them on the card. This is not for all fighters but just the ones they see hope for. They want to lock them in and make money off them. This situation really has very poor oversight and many times fighters get ripped off. They either sign a contract without getting a lawyer or their lawyer misses something. That something can be tricks and vagaries that could trap a fighter for a long time. Many a fighter in history has gone broke through these deals. Luckily, Bob looked at the contract and immediately knew that the promoter was a charlatan.

"You can't sign this. It will lock Noki up for years and even though he offers some ambiguous amounts he would pay Noki, there is nothing guaranteed. Also, he wants all pay-per-view monies and all marketing profits", said Bob.

"But we need the fight", said Bug.

"Yes, he is offering $20,000. I get that. Turn it down. He wants Noki for a reason", said Bob.

"What's that?"

"What do I know? I just know numbers. Ask Jip", Bob said.

Bug found Jip later that afternoon after a nap. The rain was hitting the gym almost as hard as the day Bug came to Carlo's.

"Hey, Jip, I got the contract".

"Great. Let me take a look?"

Bug hesitantly handed him the fax.

"Stefan Williams?" asked Jip.

"Yup", said Bug

"We were supposed to fight Dupree. What the hell is going on here? Williams is a heavyweight now".

"Yes, but I was told he just moved up. He's trying to get a name in that division. More money. They say he weighs only about 200 pounds. Lighter for today's heavyweights."

"Yeah, I know but he is good. That's our offer? Twenty thousand for an HBO fight?"

"Yup. It's from Action Boxing, I guess they do the promoting for all the fights there".

"Yes, that Stan Kotch. He owns Vegas. Been running the fights there for decades. He cannot be trusted. I've seen him bribe fighters to sign with him by buying them fancy jewelry or beautiful women and later all the money comes back out of their first paycheck. He is crook".

"So, what do we do?"

"Well, I would take the $20,000 and have Noki beat this guy and then go from there".

"Well, that's the thing. He wants a five-fight lock in."

"No, no, can't do that. Wait, what do we get in those five fights?"

"Just some guaranteed numbers. Bob says walk. It's bad."

"Do we get gate numbers? Pay-per-view?"

"Nope."

"I can't believe we finally get a miracle to get an HBO card with his losing record and we have to walk. I mean we should, right?" said Jip.

"I don't know. Maybe? I mean $20,000 would really help. And the other fight numbers do go up after that. But Bob says no."

"Well, do we have time to think about it?"

"Sure. An hour".

CHAPTER TWENTY-NINE

"Who the fuck is this?" asked Stan.

"Bug".

"I'm speaking to a bug?"

"It's a name. I help manage Noki".

"Where is Jip?"

"He wants me making these decisions. I keep him in the loop with everything. Anyway, we can take this fight for the money you offered but that's all. Noki is not signing any promotional agreements".

"Okay, then this conversation is over. Go fuck yourself", and with that, Stan hung up.

Bug was stunned but he knew these kinds of people. He knew they needed Noki or else he wouldn't have offered him the promotional agreement in the first place. Bug stared at the clock and thirty seconds later the phone rang again.

"Buck?"

"It's Bug?"

"Whatever. I'm stuck. You will rarely ever hear me admit that. I need this fight on HBO. I can't find anyone else for Williams and

HBO wants Noki fighting someone. This will be our last fight together unless the kid does a promotional contract with me."

"I understand", Bug excitedly answered.

"You understand? You understand nothing. If your kid loses, he is done anyway. If he wins then I will blacklist him afterwards. My recommendation is for you to sign that contract."

"Our lawyer says no and I can't override him".

"I thought you manage the kid?"

"I do."

"Then you're doing a shitty job. Where's Jip?"

"I told you. I will tell him, but he doesn't want the long-term agreement either."

"That old bastard needs to retire. So, you seem to be the key person in the kid's decisions, huh? Can he even understand what you are doing to him?"

"Noki trusts me".

"What are you? His conscience?"

"Sort of."

"Well, fuck it, I'm tired of talking to you. Now what is your real name?"

"Why?"

"What do you mean why? We are going to do business together. There will be legal documents drawn."

"Jim Grillo".

"Thank you. You have no accent. Where you from Mr. Hill".

"I was born in Ohio but I have been everywhere".

"What does that mean?"

"Everywhere. Atlantic City, Miami, New Orleans. Everywhere".

"Are you the midget I see with Noki?"

"I am a little person, yes."

"You look young. What are you about 35?"

"Thanks, but I am 54".

"Whatever, anyway I will send the new contract in a fax right over. I look forward to talking to you guys, especially if this kids wins".

"You got it".

And with that the conversation was over and the team got their contract and Stan Kotch got all the information he needed on Bug. It was a mistake that Bug should have seen coming.

CHAPTER THIRTY

"I don't love this idea, man", Limpy interjected. "We are putting him out of his weight class, and he could get hurt".

"But it's $20,000!" Bug answered

"I get it but is his life worth it?" Limpy asked.

"I didn't know it was that risky a fight? I thought Jip was okay with it. Noki was okay with it".

"I am", Jip said as wheeled over to the conversation. Jip could use his cane now but later in the day he was fatigued and would rely on the wheelchair for his mobility. "Williams is puffy now. He's bloated. I watched his last fight and…"

"He's slow. I can beat him", Noki spoke up as he smiled and stared into the distance while shadowboxing in the ring. No one ever knew how much Noki paid attention and this often surprised people.

"Have you seen him fight?" asked Bug.

"Today", Noki responded and moved around the ring doing an imitation of Williams. He did an imitation of a very straight up fighter throwing three jabs to one right hand with all his weight on his front foot. He then mimicked his posture, how he held his head, how he moved side to side and even how he walked back to his corner after the round was over.

"You saw him one time and remember that much?" asked Limpy.

Noki shook his head.

Most boxers don't change. They tend to fight the same way almost every time. They may adjust a little to the other fighter but it's not much. This is why different styles can be exciting for the fans but can also be boring. Unlike other sports, like football, where the teams are picked apart and analyzed looking for tendencies or "tells", boxing is a low-tech sport where trainers just wing it when they watch film. For Noki, on the other hand, it is different. He sees everything. He sees patterns, tells, tendencies, habits and everything in between. He is that high tech.

"How will you fight him?" asked Bug.

"Orlando and keep him off balance."

"Orlando?" asked Bug.

"Orlando Canizales. Yup. Great call," said Limpy, "He is my Mexican homey".

Canizales fought in the 1980s and 1990s and was bantamweight champ who defended his title sixteen times. He had an incredible way of ducking left hooks and moving under and side-to-side. His head movement and footwork were phenomenal and maybe the toughest kind of boxer ever to emulate. But not for Noki who started to move around the ring just like him.

"So, are you okay with the fight, Jip?" asked Bug.

"It's up to Noki. It's always really been up to him."

"Yes", said Noki.

"Okay, I will work with Bob to sign the contract", said Bug.

"How much are we paying him?" asked Jip.

"Who?" asked Bug.

"This guy Bob. And the rest of his crew?"

Barker, Bob and the accountant have donated their services."

"You have got to be kidding me? Honest and charitable lawyers?" asked Jip.

"We are breaking a lot of stereotypes around here, aren't we?"

"I guess we are. It sure is nice to trust some people once in a while. But lawyers? Did the world change when I had my stroke?"

"No. But I think you did", said Bug.

CHAPTER THIRTY-ONE

Kotch did not like the deal he signed and told Bug that when the team got to Las Vegas a week before the fight. The accommodations were beyond belief. The group of them were given a penthouse suite at Caesar's Palace. This was something meant for boxers in mega fights. Noki was just on the undercard so it was highly unusual.

In the room was food and games and anything anyone would ever want for a vacation, much less a boxer preparing for a fight. They had their own chef who would come in and prepare food. There was a driver to take them anywhere they wanted and during the down time the team was taken to amusement parks and shows like Cirque De Soleil. Jip didn't really do much of it and was suspicious of it all. Noki seemed to be having a grand time experiencing everything he never had even dreamed of before. Bug stayed with Noki the whole time making sure he didn't get lost in the fun and stayed on schedule. It was really the first time he had to do that with Noki.

All this did not sit well with Gideon or his team. They also had a suite, but the accommodations were more moderate. They heard about what was going on with Noki and knew it was true because they had had the same experience before they signed with Kotch. Stan was trying to impress them in order to sign them. Stan even admitted so when he was confronted by John and Gideon.

"This is my night, Stan, what the fuck is going on?" said Gideon spoke from the ring at the local Vegas gym. Kotch was checking in on his prize pupil, as he often did with the talent under his control

"Just business boys", Kotch said.

"Bullshit. I am going to destroy Johansen and then I want that fucking retard. I'll show you who the king is."

"I like that anger Lionel. You do your thing and I'll do mine."

"Why do you want Noki?" asked John.

"He is a draw. Gideon is the champ but there is more attention on Noki now because of his issues. The boxing world is buzzing".

"So, you're playing Gideon as second fiddle?"

"Now, now, that's not true at all. But I am a business man and when I see opportunities for money then I go for them".

"Just remember who the champ is, mother fucker!" said Gideon from the ring.

"Oh, I do. No worries here boys".

As Stan started to leave, John caught up to him.

"You are never going to sign him, you know", he said to Stan.

"Why would you say that?"

"I know Jip. That hard-headed asshole never gives in and I don't think he trusts you. I don't trust you."

"But you signed?"

"Yes, because to me money comes first. That's not Jip".

"Well, I have other ways to get that kid's attention. I always say, give a bad boy enough rope and he'll soon make a jackass of himself."

Chapter Thirty-Two

The weigh-in was the night before the fight. It was a circus when Noki got up to the stage. There were more fans to see him than to see his opponent. There were more fans there to see him than Gideon and his opponent. Something was different about these fans, too. Many were young and many had their own disabilities. They were autistic, or in wheelchairs, or with Down's Syndrome. Their excitement displeased the Gideon team to no end. Kotch, on the other hand, was tickled pink with excitement. He wanted to see if Noki played to the masses. He wanted to see what would happen if he put the autistic boy in the public's eye. He loved what he saw and what he saw was a goldmine.

The obligatory weigh-in stare down had a much larger Stefan Williams looking down on Noki. His weight was 206, bigger than the team thought. Noki had gotten his weight up to 181. Williams truly tried to scare Noki but, as usual, had no effect on him. Williams tried saying a few words but there was no answer from the kid. It confused Williams as the crowd screamed "Noki, Noki!"

Next, Gideon tried to make a show of his weigh-in stare down. He screamed. He flexed. He even pushed Johanson. The crowd was mildly amused, but it was definitely a letdown for the reigning champ. Something had changed. That something was Noki.

The rest of Noki's night was one of relaxation. Stan had a personal masseuse come to give him a massage. Bug had okayed it. The specialty meals were beyond amazing both that night and again the day of the fight. Bug had never been treated so well. Noki hadn't either but he didn't notice or care about the food or the massage. He did enjoy the toys, though.

A few hours before the team was to go the arena, Stan called down for Bug to see him. Jip was napping but Stan didn't want Bug to wake him. They met in the business suite of Caesar's Palace and it was just Stan there waiting.

"Hi, Mr. Hill, have we treated you well?" Stan said as Bug entered the room.

Initially taken back by his official last name, Bug finally answered with a genuine, "Yes, Mr. Kotch, this has been incredible. I can't thank you enough. Neither can the team".

"Wonderful. So, I need to talk to you about something".

"Sure, anything".

"I have some paperwork here that I need you take with you".

"Okay", Bug said hesitantly, "What's it about?"

"Well, I want to work with you. I want Noki in our stable and I need you to make that happen".

"That's really not up to me, Stan. I don't make the contract decisions. We have a lawyer that helps us with that."

"I understand but the lawyer works for you and Noki. You seem to be very important to Noki. He listens to you".

"And Jip".

"Yes, but Jip is old school. His time is done. Noki's time is now. Jip doesn't understand the nuances of how boxing works today but you do."

"I am not sure about that".

"Oh, I think you do. Your history is filled with 'experiences' that shows you understand a lot". He made quotation marks with his fingers.

"What does that mean?"

"Well, someone with all your aliases and who has been arrested multiple times, been sued multiple times for embezzlement and who has been running his whole life should know a lot about life".

Bug's heart sank. He was exposed. Stan, unlike the Texas Boxing Commission, had done his homework and hired the right people to dig up this information. Bug couldn't say a word.

"There are a lot of people looking for you. One in particular. How they hell they haven't noticed yet is beyond me. Hell, you're a damn midget."

"Little person".

"Whatever. I guess shaving your long hair and beard distracted them. Who knows? But believe me, they are coming once I tell them."

Bug was caught in a trap. He knew it. His time was up and his past was going to catch up with him. He never told Jip or Bug or Limpy his real story. They never asked.

"I'll just leave again. I'm used to that".

"Oh, I know you are, but I have the best people out there that will find you again and your enemies will find you, my little friend, no matter what. I'll make sure of it."

Bug's color left his face. He was without words.

"The contracts are on top. The second packet is all about Jim Grillo and his aliases. This is to show you that I mean business. No one needs to know about the second part. We had a hell of a time finding that out because I paid a lot of money for it. Others won't go through that trouble. Have Noki sign the contract and the second packet goes away".

"I can't sell him out. I won't", said Bug.

"Then you can say goodbye to the good life. Say goodbye to your little brainless friend. And you'll be leaving him alone to be picked apart by shadowy figures anyway."

"The lawyer will see the contract so it wouldn't matter."

"That's the beauty of it. There are two contracts. One is to make your lawyer happy. The other is to make me happy. Once the lawyer gives you the okay you have Noki and Jip sign the other one."

"You are a piece of shit, Stan, do you know that?"

"That's boxing. I'm a promoter and I collect stupid little boys to fight for me. I pay plenty of money for good prospects and people bring them to me. And then we make a lot of money together".

"You make the money".

"Yes, most of it. Sure."

"And then they never come back as boys, do they? You use them up and discard them when they serve no purpose".

"Like I always said, boxing is a bad business, for the fighters".

"It's not going to happen, Stan."

"Well, it's your choice. Listen, I don't know if he even gets past Williams tonight. But if he does then you have a week to get the deal done. And if you don't, then I expose you to Jip, Noki and your friends from your past. And I know the one you are really running from. I have done business with him before myself. He even scares me sometimes. Now get out."

Bug turned and started to walk away when Stan offered another piece of advice.

"If you truly want to help the kid, and save your hide, then get him to sign. He'll finally make some money and be taken care of. If you don't ,then he won't get another big fight. You'll get your $20,000, well much less after your expenses are taken out, but you'll get some money".

"Wait, you are making us pay for these luxuries?"

"Oh, yes, someone has to pay to live in Pleasure Island. And it won't be me. Unless, of course, you get him to sign".

Bug was flabbergasted. Stan had him by the balls and he knew it. Bug calculated that Bug may get half of what was owed and then lose more to taxes. If they came away with $5000, they would be lucky. Now he had a decision to make and with the chance of no more fights on the horizon, he knew that decision was to sacrifice himself.

Chapter Thirty-Three

TV ANNOUNCERS:

"I'm pretty excited about this fight," said Max Kellerman.

"Because of this Noki kid?" asked Jim Lampley.

"Absolutely. Williams is ranked in the top 15 for heavyweights but is not a huge guy. Noki Polendina only weighed in the low 180s so he is at a disadvantage. But the fans just want to see him box and so that his how this fight was made."

"An unfair match?" questioned Lamply.

"I'm not sure. I've seen all the tape on Noki and his style is all over the place. It's like he is imitating the great fighters of history. Truly bizarre".

"The kid does have a lot of losses on his record. Should he even be in here?"

"That's boxing. The people see who they want to see and they want more of Noki".

"Yes, the fans are filled with, well, special needs people. A different feel for a pro fight. Noki has seemed to have touched a nerve and has become somewhat of a legend or hero to these people. It's nice but…"

"Yes, but, what if he gets creamed. Is it right? Is it right for our enjoyment? I mean he has been knocked out seven times and has never fought a heavyweight before. This just seems uncomfortable. I'm uncomfortable calling the fight and I'll be a lot more uncomfortable if bad things happen".

"Well, let's hope nothing bad happens but we have no choice as I hear a roar and Noki is now coming to the ring. There is no music for his entrance".

"Strange. Everything is just strange with this kid".

"Well, let's not forget the cornermen: a little person, an invalid in a wheelchair, and someone with a terrible limp"

"I feel like I am in a circus", replied Kellerman.

"I think we are", answered Lamplcy.

Noki entered the ring, this time with a Fantasia t-shirt on. Bug was so preoccupied with his own thoughts that he didn't even comment on it. As the crowd roared, Noki started to dance around the ring, and then the music blared for the entrance of Stefan Williams. His fans were much smaller in number, which was also noted by the announcers.

After the official announcements of records and the obligatory applause for each fighter, the two fighters met again in the middle of the ring. Noki stared right through Williams but not in a menacing way. It still scared Williams.

"Okay, so, once again this is a different style for Noki," said Kellerman as the fight started.

"What's he doing, Max?" asked Lampley.

"I'm not sure yet but he is moving so smoothly. His side-to-side movements are so quick. Wow".

Noki was on his game. He circled Williams anytime he got close and moved in and out as if he was in a choreographed dance. Round one was all Noki. He only landed a few shots but Williams got in nothing. Williams' size was now a disadvantage and Noki used it against him with quickness.

Round two and three were similar. At the end of the round, Williams seemingly hit Noki with a big right hand. Williams became aggressive after that but still couldn't connect. He thought he had hurt Noki but he had not.

"Here's the replay, Max, and you can see Noki getting blasted with that right hand…wait…maybe not".

"That's an old school move. Many famous Mexican fighters would roll their head with the right head. They don't really get hit, and the damage just looks worse than it is. Actually, there is no damage".

"You don't see that much anymore, huh, Max?"

"Orlando Canizales! That's who Noki is fighting as. The great bantamweight champ. Oh, man, I knew it".

"But how does he change each time and imitate great fighters so well?"

"I have no idea."

By round six, Williams was done. He was a bloated light heavyweight, who was pretending to be a heavyweight, and could not catch a speedy and lighter fighter. He couldn't breathe by the end of the round and Noki was literally spinning around him. He was picking Williams apart and then the blood started to come out his nose and left eye. A slow left hook was his last punch and Noki rolled under it, moved to his right and blasted Williams in the left temple with his own right hand. He was able to beat the count, and beat the bell, but he would not come out for the seventh round. Another very good fighter disposed of by Noki Polendina.

When the ref told Noki's corner the fight was over there was celebration by the crew, but Bug had lost a little zip in his step. His mind was somewhere else. If Noki would have lost then there would be no interest by Stan to sign him. And no one would care about Bug's past. But now the fans were intrigued even more. The autistic boy who can mimic other great champions had the world's attention, even non-boxing fans. This made Stan Kotch salivate.

Max Kellerman was able to interview Noki in the ring almost as well as Teddy Atlas did, which means poorly.

"You looked great, Noki, congratulations", said Max

Noki just shook his head and Bug said "Thanks, Max".

"Noki, it looks like you were fighting like Orlando Canizales. Is that right?"

Noki shook his head again. Kellerman had not realized giving Noki a closed- ended question, that could be answered with a yes or no, was a mistake.

"Okay, well, how did you learn to do that?"

"Watching".

"So....you watch these fighters and then imitate them?"

Noki should his head again.

"Okay, one more thing, what's next for Noki Polendina?"

Noki was confused then answered, "Shower?".

"No, I mean careerwise?"

"We have big plans and hope to come here and work with the Action Boxing Group", said Bug. Limpy was next to Bug and had a confused expression on his face. Jip stayed out of the ring in his wheelchair, so he didn't hear the comment. The main event, Gideon vs. Johansen, was about to come on next so the Kellerman quickly ended the interview.

Bug was not sure why he said it. He knew they had to work with Kotch's group in some manner but maybe he blurted it out just to buy himself some time. Maybe he could make some scenario work. If Noki signs the bad contract and gets the multi-fight deal then at least he gets some money. If he doesn't then Bug is a dead man and Noki is blackballed. That was how powerful Stan Kotch was. It was already messing with Bug's head.

Bug was lost in thought as all the scenarios went through his head. As they sat in the locker room getting prepared to leave, they could hear the roar of the next fight going on. It was Gideon doing his business once again with a first-round knockout.

Bug truly wanted to find an answer to his dilemma. There must be a way to protect Noki and the team from hearing about his past and yet still get the payday that the team needed. That's all that Bug thought about from that point until they returned home by plane the next day.

Chapter Thirty-Four

The week following the fight was one of the hardest yet to control as far as crowds. Between the media attention from the trial and then his knock out in a potentially lucrative new weight division, Noki was starting to become a mini celebrity. People wanted to come see this oddity, who could imitate any boxer. The size of the gym made Carlo's Gym too hot and uncomfortable. This was becoming an issue and Bug had to figure out a system for visitors. Weirdly enough, this made more white-collar boxers sign up to learn boxing with Limpy, mainly as a way to brag that they worked out in the same gym as Noki.

"Bug, you got a second,", asked Jip.

"Yes, sir", Bug answered.

"What's the plan?"

"For….."

"Noki?"

"I am not really sure. I was told that he is now ranked in the top ten in the light heavyweight division and top twenty in the heavyweight division", Bug said.

"I knew it. This opens up all new possibilities. But we don't want to fight heavyweight and we sure as hell don't want to fight Gideon".

"Why not?"

"Because Gideon is a stone-cold killer, that's why. And heavyweights are just too big".

"So, we don't want a championship fight?" asked Bug.

"I'm not sure. Stan has other fighters we can beat. Let's just make a little money to pay our debts and be comfortable and get the hell out of the business".

"I don't think it's that easy", replied Bug.

"Sure it is. Listen, I don't think I can handle my son getting hurt. We are getting to another level of skill here. Now we are getting to the great fighters. Noki may not be able to pull this off any longer."

"We have received some offers out of the country for Noki. It's for heavyweight fights, though."

Limpy slowly moved towards the conversation and chimed in, "I don't know, man, Williams was a small heavyweight. We don't want to touch those guys who are 250 lbs and 6'6".

"I agree", said Bug.

"Of course, no way he fights heavyweight. We will just use it for leverage. Stan must have sent a contract with his check, right? "said Jip.

"He gave me the contract but no check".

"What? That son-of-a-bitch. So, what is the contract for?"

"It's a five-fight deal".

"No way. He will abuse Noki. Nope, not going to happen".

"It's $50k for the first and the doubles each time to max out at $800,000".

"That's a lot, Jip", said Limpy.

Bug realized that Jip didn't understand how much Noki would be losing. The contract, different than what the lawyer was seeing, was garbage. It was a set-up to fight Gideon and if he won then Noki would be paraded around for more fights, all the while making very little. And no one thought Noki could truly beat Gideon. The sparring session they had was just that, sparring. Gideon mangled his opponents and Bug knew he would be tossing his friend in with a lion. There also was the issue of Stan Kotch, a disgusting creep who manipulated, lied, cheated and….

It was then that Bug realized why he hated Stan so much. Stan was just a bigger and more successful version of himself. A parasite who did nothing but suck off the ideas and successes of others. He and Stan were users. With a little effort Bug knew he could convince Jip that Stan's deal was the right one. He would lie to them and say the lawyer made the appropriate changes and give them the second contract. They wouldn't know the difference and Bug would be home scot free. They didn't need to find out what Stan discovered about

Bug's past. He didn't need to share with Jip, Limpy or Noki about his past crimes. And Stan wouldn't blacklist them.

Bug was in a dilemma. He was stuck. He could tell everyone the truth, about the contract and his past, and run away or push the garbage contract through and try to get away with it. In the past it wouldn't be a hard decision for him. He had always done what he had need to do to survive and take care of himself. No one looked after him, so he did what he had to do, without any regrets. He had always only thought about one thing and that was saving himself. But that was the old Jim Grillo. He needed to resolve this conundrum by talking to the only person he trusted.

CHAPTER THIRTY-FIVE

"I am glad you are telling me all this, but I really don't know what to say", said Fay.

"I am a loser. That is all I have ever been. I have done terrible things to other bad people and now they are catching up with me. All I have ever cared about is me", said Bug.

"Will passing off the bad contract save you?"

"It will save my life but not my soul. But who am I kidding anyway? I'm a little person and there are not many of us in the boxing world. Eventually my past would have caught up with me even though I look different without the hair and the beard".

"So why not come clean?" asked Fay.

"If I do that then they won't sign the contract. They just won't. And then I am probably a dead man and Noki may never get another fight anyway. Everyone loses".

"But you will be free".

This resonated with Bug. It was what he needed to hear. But then he thought better of it.

"Free but dead".

"No, we don't want that. There has to be another way".

"No, you were right the first time. I need to stop running because that was is no way to live. I need to take care of Noki, that's all that matters. That's the only way to find peace. I need to face my own demons".

"I can't answer this for you, Bug. I don't want you to get hurt. Maybe, after you fess up to your past to these people who you love, you just leave again? Run. Hide. You have done so much for Noki and put them in a position to succeed. Maybe your time with them is up. I don't know. All I know is that you have shown yourself to be brave, truthful and unselfish. If that was a test then you have passed it. There has to be some karma to that?"

"I don't know. Maybe. But I am not running. Not anymore".

CHAPTER THIRTY-SIX

It was the hardest discussion that he ever had to make. Before the next day's workout, he sat down with Noki, Jip and Limpy and confessed everything. He detailed his past and the people who were looking for him. He explained the double contract and the extortion by Stan. With tears in his eyes ,he apologized for everything and gave his resignation. He wanted no money for managing Noki and offered to sign off on everything in front of Barker or Bob so it would be official. He was a loser, he told them, who had poisoned their lives.

The group was stunned, except Noki. He just stared, barely looking like he was even paying attention. It was Jip who spoke up.

"Well, I had my doubts about you when you came here. I should have known".

Bug just stared at the floor. As Jip was going to say something else, Noki got up and went over to Bug and hugged him. He had to get on his knees to do it. He had never hugged anyone before like this. It was a real hug. This did not go unnoticed by Jip.

"You're my friend. Please don't leave", said Noki, who started to cry, an emotion rarely seen by Jip.

Jip scratched the little hair he had left on his head and said, "Well, no one is innocent in this sport. No one. And no one goes through life without making mistakes. The time you spent with us has only been good and you made our lives better. Most importantly, Noki needs you. So, I need you."

"Thank you, Jip, but it's not so easy. Bad people are coming for me".

"So? How bad could they be? I have seen everything in this business".

"Well, when you take from these people, they take your life".

"Yeah, that's bad".

"And if you don't sign Stan's contract then he will blacklist Noki and no more fights".

"Ah, bullshit. You see those people out there?" Jip pointed to the massive crowds trying to see Noki work out.

"Yes", said Bug.

"There are thousands more who want to see him fight. Hundreds of thousands. That means money. That's all that Stan wants."

"But Stan said no chance."

"If I know Gideon, and I do, he won't stand for it. I know for a fact that he cannot handle Noki getting all the attention. He will want that fight and force Stan's hand".

"But you don't want him fighting Gideon. The risk is too high".

"It is but I have an idea. Maybe we negotiate a one fight deal for Gideon for a decent payday. And just maybe Noki gets hit with a weak shot and gets knocked out. No one could make it look better than him. No one would be the wiser. Gideon gets his pride back. Noki walks away healthy. We get paid and stop this boxing crap forever."

"Brilliant. We do the Bruce "The Mouse" Strauss thing again. Noki, are you okay with that?"

Noki shrugged his shoulders in a very noncommittal way.

"Bug, you are going to have to stay close to us the whole training camp. We have to move you into our section of the house. I have my shotgun but it's an antique musket and I am not even sure I can hold it so well".

Bug knew this was the only way he could live without running away. Maybe if he never left the group, he could survive through the training camp and then the fight. He just hoped it wasn't a mistake.

CHAPTER THIRTY-SEVEN

Stan pulled all the contracts once Bug told him. He screamed and shouted on the phone. He told them they were done boxing. When he hung up, he immediately told his people to alert Bug's enemies as to his whereabouts.

A few days passed after the phone call. Bug was now in the main house and slept on the floor next to Noki. He had his bags packed ready to run at a moment's notice. Jip had his old shotgun next to him in case of emergency but Bug didn't feel that safe. In fact, Jip probably wouldn't hear an intruder over his snoring. During regular hours Bug hung around the gym and could not stop himself from inspecting everyone who entered the facility. He was getting paranoid but he didn't leave.

Jip was right about the demand for Noki. The press was hounding Gideon who was negotiating a fight with another contender. Why wouldn't he fight Noki? Was he afraid of him? Was he ducking him? This did not sit well with the champ who let Stan know that he in no uncertain terms thathe wouldn't fight anyone else but Noki. Now it was Stan who was cornered. He needed his star pupil to fight and make him money. He tried to convince the press that they were wrong about Gideon. He tried to convince Gideon to move on, but he would have none of it. Stan needed to make the fight with Noki happen and so he called Bug.

"Okay, you little shit, the fight is on. I will send over a one-contract deal".

"And my life?"

"What do I care about you? You made your bed. Now sleep in it. I had my people tell those friends of yours and there is nothing I can do now. I think your time is up".

"Yeah, I guess so. Stan, I guess I'll get mine. I deserve it. But then again, maybe you deserve some karma too".

"Ha. karma. I own this town. I own the boxing world. Just have that little idiot sign the contract and if I see you again, which I probably won't, then we'll both have a drink to karma".

The contract came through a few minutes later. If Noki were to lose then he would get a payday for that fight but nothing else. If he were to win, then he would be world champion and be free to fight anytime or anywhere without being shackled to Stan Kotch. Bob and Barker both looked it over at their office and said it was good to go.

But there was no way Stan could let Noki win so he had a plan to make sure Gideon could not lose. Sure, he controlled the judges so a decision going against Gideon was not going to happen. Stan was a crook and he was greedy, and he hatched another scheme that would guarantee his pupil's victory.

The contract was sent back via all the appropriate signatures. The phone then rang again.

"You got your way, Samuel", said Stan on the phone.

"Thanks", Bug replied.

"You'll pay for it, though".

"I am sure I will. Whatever happens to me is fine. I am at peace with that. You need to leave Noki alone, though."

"I won't be needing the retard after this is done, you little shit", Stan said as he hung up the phone.

"What did he say?" asked Limpy.

"Well, we need to make sure the plan is in play for Noki. I have a bad feeling about what Stan is going to make Gideon do."

"No worries, homey, Noki will do his trick and we are out. With that cash and the white-collar boxing business, we should be set.

"Great", said Bug. But he wasn't so sure.

Bug caught up with Noki that night while watching films of Gideon. Noki was studying hard, which surprised Bug just a little. He also had all the manuals out with notes he had written about Gideon. These were the first things he showed Bug when they met.

"I appreciate how much you are preparing, Noki. How will you do it?"

"Do what?"

"Go down?"

Noki just shrugged his shoulders. That was not like him. When they first started fighting, he would mime exactly how his "dive" would look. He was not doing that now. This worried Bug.

CHAPTER THIRTY-EIGHT

The fight was two months away and Noki went about his training camp like he normally would. All sparring occurred behind closed doors with no public to watch and especially no cameras. They had to make the ruse looked good and Noki would do his regular routine. So as not to get hurt, the team decided that Noki would fight like Sugar Ray Leonard. Leonard was a master in the ring. When he didn't let his ego get in the way, by going toe-to-toe with fighters, he was almost unhittable. He danced and moved like a smaller Muhammed Ali, but without the rope a-dope. He was a ballerina with gloves and he used his speed and agility to move around the ring as if it were his dominion. Noki became him in training as he prepared for the toughest fight of his life.

"How will he do it, Jip?" asked Bug.

"It's his call. It would look better if he could survive about three rounds to give the fans their money worth. Then he could make a weak shot look like a cannon hit him and fold like a lawn chair".

"Does that bother you?"

"Yes and no. I hate John. I hate Gideon. But it's not worth Noki getting hurt. Hell, boxing isn't worth it. Let's just get the hell out of the business, take our money, save Noki and move on".

"I'm okay with that. Is Noki?"

"He hasn't said anything to me, so I guess so".

But Bug wasn't so sure. Noki was training hard but then again, he always did. And Noki always did what he was told. He always tended to business. Bug knew he didn't like Gideon but Noki wasn't like normal people. He didn't let his ego destroy him. He let things go. Maybe he was just being paranoid, Bug thought.

After two press conferences, both of them being fiascos as Noki would not say anything, they were only a week away from the fight. No one had come for Bug who by this time who was starting to let his guard down. He made it through training camp and now they were off to Las Vegas. This time they were treated very differently by Stan.

CHAPTER THIRTY-NINE

The fight was to be held at Caesar's Palace again and the accommodations for Gideon and his crew were top notch. They had the penthouse and received all the amenities that Noki had for his last fight. For Noki, this was not the case. They were put up in a rundown Motel 5 down the block. Yes, Motel 5, a knock off of the famous brand. Things had definitely changed. There was no chef, no massages and no quality rooms. There were plenty of roaches though.

Jip was not happy. Sure, the hotel and living situation were terrible but the gym situation was worse. Noki had to use a second-rate gym out of town, and only at odd hours, which switched daily during the week. All of this as revenge for the team not signing a multi-fight contract with Stan. It was also a method for getting inside a fighter's head but Noki would have none of that. The situation didn't bother him as he went about his business, training as hard as he ever had.

"Jip, is Noki on the same page as us?" asked Bug.

"Why?"

"Because he is training awfully hard for someone who is going to take a dive."

"I get that. And shut your mouth. If anyone hears that then we won't even get a dime out of this fight. Not a word".

"I get it, but does he?"

"Listen, ever since this kid started in the gym, he only knew one thing and that is to train hard. He doesn't think about it. He doesn't question things like you and me. He doesn't burn out. He just knows routines and this is his routine".

This made sense to Bug. Maybe he was giving too much thought to the situation. Maybe Noki was just that simple and really didn't stress over anything. Something just seemed odd about him.

The night before the fight was the weigh-in. The crowd was as immense as it was the last time Noki was in Las Vegas. In fact, it was even bigger. Media from all over the world was interested in this title fight. There were too many angles to play that would tug at their audiences' hearts: the mean fighter versus the autistic one, the loser who turned his career around, or the misfits that took over the boxing world. On and on it went.

Noki weighed in first at 174 lbs. He had shed some weight since his last fight but that wasn't hard. He never acknowledged the audience after the weight was announced. He just got off the scale and went to his team. Jip and Limpy were there but Bug was missing. They had looked for him and called him and he was not to be found. Noki was a little shaken, a first for him, and Jip noticed. Jip was bothered too but knew he had to take care of things. He just thought that Bug had decided it was time to save his own hide and run. And Jip could understand that.

Gideon came on to the stage screaming, and he had a massive entourage with him. Not only was Stan and John with him, but also a whole force of friends, cling-ons, security men and so on. There was a mixture of boos and cheers as his weight was announced. It was 175 lbs. on the nose. Gideon screamed. He flexed his muscles. It was like a live peacock on stage.

After coming off the scale, the two fighters were brought together for a final stare down and photo opportunity. Gideon tried to intimidate Noki by saying things like,

"You ain't shit, motherfucker", "I am going to make you more retarded", " You're going home in a shorter bus" and on and on. None of this bothered Noki as he stared right through Gideon. He was thinking only of one thing. Where was his friend?

CHAPTER FORTY

It had only been hours before the weigh in when Bug had decided to get a drink in the lobby. He had needed to calm his nerves. He never got that drink. Two large men had whisked him away in their black Lincoln Continental. Bug didn't fight. He knew is time was up. These were not ordinary men. These were gangsters. They never said anything more than, "Come with us", and that is all they needed to say.

The drive took over thirty minutes. Bug could see, through the window, a star shining over the mountains. It was the same star he had seen almost a year earlier when he asked for help. He thought of the cruel irony that this was to be the last thing he sees. It was only when they pulled into the parking lot did Bug start to get confused. Getting to the desert takes more time than that and the desert is the best place to bury someone if you don't want them found again. Bug's confusion was cleared up when he saw the light green Cadillac with the white roof in the driveway. It was Pepe Grillo's car.

Then Bug saw a building. The restaurant was a flashback to the old days of Vegas when organized crime ran the town. The furniture was old and run down but still had a semblance of the decadence it used to have. It was darkly lit and full of smoke. There were no slot machines here, just men talking at tables as they ate. Bug and his captors moved him through the restaurant to the back room. No one eating even looked up. There sat Pepe at the table smoking his cigar.

"We meet again, you little bastard", Pepe said.

"Yes, we meet again. I guess you want to tell me something before you kill me?" asked Bug.

"Yes, I thought you were ugly before with your beard and long hair but somehow you actually look worse. How is that even possible?" His two henchman started to laugh.

"Is that it? You wantto mock me first? Like I don't get that every day of my life? Okay, great, I look worse. Let's just get this done".

"Not so fast. You owe me money. And I want my money."

"I don't have it so you may as well kill me". Bug could have tried to beg for his life by telling Pepe that he would get a good amount of cash after this fight. But he knew that Pepe would just take that money and kill him later anyway so why not let Noki keep it all?

"It's not that easy. You see, you should have been dead a few weeks ago but someone saved your life and offered us a deal."

Bug was totally confused. Who would save him? Who would make a deal for his life? Just then he heard a flush from the toilet attached to the room. It broke the silence in an embarrassing way. A few seconds later, he could hear someone huffing and puffing and then a massive human being exited the bathroom.

"Hello, Bug", said Frank Calzone.

"You are my savior?" asked Bug

"I am nobody's savior. It just behooves me that you stick around a while and help this kid win. Pepe and I have a mutual respect and understanding. We are not going to change that for you."

"What does that mean?"

"That means you still owe me my money!" yelled Pepe.

"Yes, you still owe him that money plus the vig", Frank broke it, "You can't get out of that. He is just not going to kill you and still take the money. In fact, I have paid him for you so now you owe me that money plus the vig".

"Thanks, Frank"

"Don't thank me yet. You need to promise me one thing. This kid of yours is now a 4 to 1 underdog. He needs to win. I am betting a lot on him."

"Ummm.....Gideon is a great fighter, Frank, I can't...."

"Bullshit. You have been magical for this kid. Make this happen and all is forgotten. Well, after you pay your debt to me. You see, I convinced Pepe to bet on Noki too. I told him that his earlier losses were dives. This kid wins tomorrow and we are all happy and we will be all even. This kid loses and I cannot protect you anymore. In fact, then I kill you".

"So he wins and I am free forever?"

"Yes", said Frank. "Pepe?"

"Yes, I will spare your life on those conditions. Now get this little midget out of here. And someone close that bathroom door. My God, Frank".

CHAPTER FORTY-ONE

"Where the hell were you?" asked Limpy.

"I was preoccupied", replied Bug.

"What the hell does that mean", said Jip rolling up to him in his wheelchair.

Noki had gone to bed after all the excitement and the three of them were in the lobby of the Motel 5. It was an awkward meeting and Bug decided to fess up.

"Those people I told you about. Well, they are here."

"And?" asked Jip.

"They are giving me a chance. I just need to pay up after the fight".

"That's all? Then it's over?" asked Jip.

"Yes", said Bug. He neglected to tell them that Noki needs to win. He couldn't do it. He knew it was over for him. The best thing was to stick with the plan. Noki didn't need to get hurt trying to beat Gideon. And the only way to beat him was to go toe-to-toe with him. From the beginning he was told that by Noki himself. Bullies like Gideon need to be backed up and out-bullied. That was not the plan they had in place. The plan now was to be Sugar Ray Leonard and outbox him, move around and then take a small hit and make it look like it was a knockout blow. Bug was ready to sacrifice himself for the kid and he felt at peace with it. He was finally being unselfish and it actually felt good.

Bug slept well that night. There was no more looking over his shoulder. He had confronted his past and dealt with it. His end was near, but it didn't matter. He was in it for the greater good and that was to take care of Noki, Jip and even Limpy.

The next morning, which was the day of the fight, the team stayed at the motel just relaxing. Noki was extremely happy to have Bug back and they relaxed by watching boxing videos on the computer. Most of those fights were of Gideon and almost all of them ended in vicious knockouts. Noki was also consulting his manuals he had brought with him.

"You are all set to do the right thing?"

"I know what the right thing is", replied Noki who stared into Bug's eyes.

"Are you sure?"

"Are you?"

"Noki, I can't go round and round with you on this. I need you to be taken care of. Please tell me you will be alright?"

"Yes, I will be good. Now I save everyone. That is how the story goes."

"What story?"

"My life story".

Bug was perplexed by his last statement, but before he could respond the conversation ended when Limpy entered the hotel room. "It's time to go, amigos".

Bug was not ready for the melee ahead of them. Caesar's Palace was jam packed. When their van pulled up there was a massive crowd waiting for them. It was not a normal boxing crowd as there were all sorts of fans in wheelchairs and with different disabilities waiting to cheer their hero. Noki was now the poster boy for the physically and mentally oppressed. One child gave Noki a t-shirt and Noki looked at it and kept it. It was a sweet reminder of who he was fighting for, which made it only tougher to swallow the fact that he was planning on faking a knockout.

The team made their way to the dressing room and waited while the undercard fights went on. It was quiet, with an occasional roar from the crowd. Not long after, the fight inspector and John came in to inspect Noki's hand wraps before the fight. This is standard to make sure there is no improprieties going on. Jip just stared at John as Limpy finished the wraps. It was all he could do to control himself and not attack him. When they were done, and the inspector literally put his signature on each wrapping, Limpy went with the inspector and John to watch Gideon being wrapped.

Limpy returned about twenty minutes later and helped Noki start to warm up. He shadow boxed in the locker room for a while and then began hitting the hand pads. A few minutes later an attendant came in to tell them it was time to make their way into the ring. Bug looked at his pocket watch, which said 10:02. The same time that Noki always did his night training in the past. Noki asked to wear the shirt he was given earlier. It was a bright yellow shirt with the Special Olympics insignia on the front. On the back was their famous saying, "Let me win. But if I cannot win, let me be brave in the attempt."

This did not go unnoticed by Bug.

CHAPTER FORTY-TWO

"Here comes Noki Polendina. The fans are going crazy. What is that song he is coming in to?" said Joe, the TV announcer.

"I have no idea", replied Teddy Atlas.

"I think it is a Disney song. Wait…um…yes…it's *When You Wish Upon a Star*".

"Interesting choice for this man-child. I hope he gets his wish tonight because Lionel Gideon is no cartoon. He is the real deal. A dream killer."

Noki entered the ring with Bug and Limpy. In the front row Bug could see all the celebrities. He also saw Frank and Pepe. It was a surreal combination of stars and gangsters and everything in between. The crowd in the more distant rows were made up of the same people who had met them earlier. They were an eclectic bunch who were there to cheer on their hero. Bug noticed Fay, the social worker who was always looking out for them. She was easy to pick out with her blue outfit. They made sure she had a ticket and they were so happy to see she was there. Bug felt bad because he did not tell her the plan, but he knew she would be invaluable in consoling Noki later.

Noki was oblivious to them all. His tunnel vision focus never changed. What was once his weakness in his real life was now an advantage. Nothing bothered him. At least yet.

"Here comes Gideon and his entourage", said Joe to the television audience. The lights got dark and then the spotlight was put on the champion while he walked toward the ring. Rap music was blaring from the speakers.

"This guy is a true brawler, Joe. His intense expression says it all. He looks like he is not happy to be here and wants to end his opponent", said Atlas.

"And he usually does, Teddy."

The loud rap music to which Gideon entered continued until he was in the ring. He never stopped staring at Noki, but Noki never noticed. The crowd erupted as Michael Buffer announced Noki's name and record. There was a less of a cheer for Gideon, which made him even more mad.

The two went into the middle of the ring for the last instructions by the referee. Gideon never took his eyes off Noki and Noki responded by staring right through him like he wasn't even there. "Retards can't fight. Be a man and let's do this, bitch", Gideon said exactly as he had said in their sparring match a long time ago,

The fight was on.

Limpy and Bug, as usual, had the corner duties. Jip had his cane with him to get out of the wheelchair when he could, but he was placed at the base of the stairs going into the ring. He was unable to get out and get to the corner and tell Noki his thoughts. Noki would just need to look down to hear it.

"Stick with the plan, son. Be Sugar Ray. Tend to business. I am proud of you and I love you", said Jip.

Noki shook his head and gave a smile.

"Here we go", said Joe as the bell rang for the first round.

Gideon charged fast as he normally does and began throwing haymakers, which missed wildly as Noki ducked, spun and danced around the room.

"Noki, once again, is fighting a different style. This kid is amazing. I don't know how you prepare for him".

"Who is he fighting as, Teddy?" asked Joe.

"It looks like Sugar Ray. Yes, he is doing the shuffle with his feet. And there is the windmill with his right hand. This kid is unbelievable".

Noki threw jabs and then moved in and out as not to get hit. Gideon's adrenaline was working against him as he kept lunging and jumping to catch Noki. All was going to plan until Gideon caught Noki in the corner and grabbed him. The referee tried to break it up but Gideon would have none it. He hit Noki with small shots to the side of the head and ear. And Noki went down. It looked like he slipped but he didn't.

Bug saw Noki fall and knew it was all over. He just figured he had taken the dive earlier but that was okay. The kid was going to go home with money in his pocket, the gym would be saved and the whole fiasco would be over. So, would he. He looked over at Jip who had a confused expression on his face. Bug turned back to the ring and saw Noki getting up. He was going to continue fighting. This puzzled Bug. Was Noki really hurt? The round ended shortly thereafter and Noki came back to the ring.

"Teddy, the replay shows these shots by Gideon were not much. Maybe Noki does have a glass chin?"

"I guess so. I mean these were short little blows but their damage was impressive".

"The kid is hurt and you can see his face is swelling up there."

"Not sure this will last any longer", replied Teddy.

There was chaos in the corner. Limpy was putting the endswell on Noki's face to control the swelling under his left eye. Bug whispered to Noki, "I thought we had a plan?"

"I want to win. This is my story."

"Yes, I know, Noki, but you have nothing to prove."

"I don't like him", said Noki.

"I know. No one does. Stick to the plan and let's go home".

"He's cheating".

"What?" asked Bug.

"He's cheating!" exclaimed Noki.

The ten second warning buzzer went off as Noki stood. Bug told him to move around and grab tight if he holds again.

The second round was similar to the first with Noki moving well. He regained his wits and capitalized on all of Gideon's weaknesses.

"C'mon, bitch. Stand here and fight", said Gideon.

Noki would have none of it.

It's obvious that after all the years of torment that he knew Gideon inside and out. He saw everything he was going to do before Gideon did it. With a minute left in the round Gideon was able to smother Noki against the ropes. Once again, he began to mangle Noki with small shots to any part of the body and head that was open. Noki tried to grab his arms but to no avail. It was a street brawl with only one person doing the brawling. And the referee did nothing. He was obviously told not to by Stan. With thirty seconds left in the round ,Noki took a knee to get a break from the beating and took a standing eight count. By this time, his ear, nose and cheek were bleeding. He left eye was swelling badly. Noki was able to continue and he survived until the bell rang.

"Teddy, this is a massacre. I think I see fans crying in the stands."

Fay was one of them. She held her face in her hand and only was able to sneak a peek now and then.

"The referee needs to think about stopping this", Teddy replied, "These small shots are doing so much damage and Noki cannot handle it. He is starting to get really hurt in there".

In Noki's corner the chaos continued. Limpy, working as the cutman, tried to control the bleeding by keeping the endswell on his cheek.

"Noki, I think I need to stop this. I know you are not going to quit now but I can't let this continue", said Bug.

"But why?" replied Noki.

"Because I need to protect you", replied Bug.

"No. I save you. That is how this goes. Besides, he is cheating!"

"I don't think he is cheating. It's a brawl. That's what he does."

"No, he's cheating. Margarito".

"What?"

"Margarito".

The ten second buzzer rang and Noki stood up. The ref asked if he was okay and he nodded his head.

"What did he say?", Jip asked Bug from down below.

"He said Margarita".

"What?"

209

"He said he wants a Margarita".

Jip was confused. And then it dawned on him.

"That fucker is cheating! There is something wrong with his wraps. He put something in them!" screamed Jip.

In 2009, before his title fight with Shane Mosely, a fighter name Antonio Margarito was caught with illegal hand wraps containing gypsum which, when combined with moisture, forms plaster of Paris. He was basically trying to fight with a cast on his hands to cause more damage. This brought into question whether he had done this before, especially when he inflicted terrible damage to Miguel Cotto, a much better opponent. This stunt is easily pulled off by rewrapping the fighters hands after the inspector leaves and forging his signature on them.

Before the bell rang, Jip could see John laughing in the opposing corner. Without hesitation, Jip rolled his wheelchair around the ring towards John and start hitting him with his cane. The bell rang but the round was postponed a few seconds into it by the referee. There was a scuffle in Gideon's corner. Stan, not far from the team in the front row as well, had a grin from ear-to-ear. His plan was working perfectly. If he couldn't have Noki, then no one would. Each fighter stayed in their corner as security came and grabbed Jip. It was a circus.

"You son-of-a-bitch. You cheating bastard. You can't win fair and square? You had to pull a fast one. Now you're done!" screamed Jip.

John just laughed and turned to Stan who also had a smile on his face.

"This is crazy Teddy", said Joe, "Noki's father is attacking the opposing cornerman. What the heck is going on!"

"I'm not sure. He is yelling something about cheating. This is unbelievable!" exclaimed Atlas.

Bug had no answers for Noki. Noki was wounded and staring at his father being escorted away. Bug also saw Jip, who was fighting the security men, being wheeled out of the building. Jip bought himself some time as he dropped his cane and screamed for the security to get it. He looked up at his poor son staring at him and said one word, "Tyson".

Bug didn't understand at first but Noki did. It was the one fighter than Noki had promised never to emulate again. Noki looked confused, but Jip said it again as he was being wheeled off.

"Noki, it's okay now. It's your time. Fight fire with fire. Tyson. I am permitting you to do it. Tend to business". It was the last thing he said as security took him past the fans into the locker room.

"Fighters ready?", the ref asked.

Noki looked at Bug. "You heard your father. Tyson".

Noki smiled and his demeanor changed. His stance and posture changed. He became Mike Tyson, just like he did years earlier when he first hurt other sparring partners.

"Here we go for what seems to be the last round for Noki. No way he makes it through this fight", said the television announcer.

"I agree, Joe, but wait. He is going right after Gideon. He is fighting differently again. I know that style. That's Iron Mike", said Atlas who had actually been an ex-trainer of the former heavyweight champ.

Before Gideon could even get a few steps out of his corner, Noki came right at him just as Mike Tyson would. With lethal blows meant to kill, Noki began backing Gideon up to the ropes. Gideon was not used to going backwards and his weaknesses showed. Noki began throwing punch after punch. Left hooks to body, a weakness of Gideon's. Upper cuts that split his defense perfectly. Noki was a man possessed. He kept hitting Gideon until Gideon went to his left knee and the referee had to give him an eight count. The champ was in trouble. He knew it. John knew it. Stan knew it. And they were worried.

"I can't believe what I am seeing. What a turnaround. Lionel Gideon is badly hurt. Can Noki Polendina finish him?"

Noki was in the neutral corner staring at Gideon. Gideon looked back with the pitiful expression of a wounded animal. It was Noki's choice at this point. He could do whatever he wanted. He could just throw a couple of easy punches proving that Gideon was defenseless or he could put the bully out of his misery. It turns out that he didn't always ignore those years of abuse by his opponent. With a fifteen-punch barrage, Noki pummeled Gideon so badly that the referee had to drag him off of him.

"You're a cheater!" Noki screamed at Gideon, who was now lying on the floor, "Why?"

The fight was over and the stadium erupted. It was Limpy who grabbed the boxing commissioner to bring him to Gideon's corner. As much as John tried to hide the hand wraps, after pulling off his gloves and cutting them off his fighter's fists, it was not enough. The commissioner was able to grab them and feel the hardened mass.

Michael Buffer announced the winner. Gideon was not there for post-fight interview due to his injuries. He was taken back by his team but the commissioner and security went with them. There was going to be hell to pay for the hand wraps.

"What's next for Noki Polendina?" asked Teddy Atlas, who did not know about the wraps at that time. The team , all except for Jip, was in the middle of the ring for the television interview.

Stan Kotch jumped in as if he was part of Noki's team and said, "We are going to make Noki a star and bring him all around the world".

Noki pushed Stan away and said, "I don't like you".

Teddy was taken aback by the mini altercation.

"Noki, you are the light heavyweight champion of the world, what do you want to do next?" Teddy asked, who was speaking into the public microphone so the whole arena could hear the conversation.

"I want to go to Disney World."

The fans erupted and Noki left the ring to be with his father.

CHAPTER FORTY-THREE

After the parade ended, the group was surrounded by adoring fans. They were all there, in the Magic Kingdom, celebrating Noki's victory. It was now a week after the fight. After spending some time with his fans, Noki grabbed Bug and led them to an area he wanted to show them. Jip and Limpy followed along. Noki seemed to know exactly where he wanted to go, but with all the people wanting his autograph it just took a long time to get there. Noki's memory of the place was uncanny as he had only been there once as a boy. But this was typical of his memory. The Walt Disney World staff, used to bringing celebrities around, were trying to block off many of Noki's fans but Noki would have none of it. As they made their way past the Haunted Mansion, which was on their left, Noki kept pulling Bug in the direction of Cinderella's Castle. The parade had left the group off near Adventureland, where Bug had made the comment that Limpy, with the way he moves, would fit right in with the other animatronics in the Pirates of the Caribbean. This prompted Limpy's comeback line, about five minutes later, as they passed It's A Small World. "Looks like they have a place for you too, homey." That only received a grunt from Bug. Only a few feet later, Noki just stopped.

"Noki, the Castle is straight ahead. Don't you want to see it?" asked Jip.

"No, Papa, I want to go in here", Noki replied as he turned left towards a place that was not even a ride. At this point the fans again crowded Noki. They were not easy to miss, this "cripple crew", and even nonboxing fans now knew of the only autistic boxing champ ever. Noki took some more pictures and the Disney staff asked if he wanted their help to get them to the castle.

"No, I want to go in here", as he pointed to the small fast food restaurant.

"Are you hungry, Noki?" asked Bug.

"No. Come with me", said Noki.

The crew walked in with the Disney staff helping keep other fans from coming inside. Noki stopped in a small alcove of the restaurant seating area and sat down.

"Oh, you want a rest? I get it", said Bug

Fans were now peering in the glass from the outside and filling up the windows. Noki paid no attention. As he sat there staring there was an eerie silence as Noki just kept smiling. It was Bug who broke that silence.

"Noki, we have been contacted for a rematch. There are some other major fights being offered to us as well."

"I don't want to anymore."

"What? You don't want to fight? Don't you want to defend your belt."

"But why?"

"Because that is what champions do".

Noki just shrugged his shoulders.

"We are going in circles here. I thought you liked boxing. "

"I did. But now everything is fixed. I saved us."

"So now you don't want to box anymore?"

"I don't know. But I like it here."

"Everyone loves Disney World."

"Yes, but right here."

"In this restaurant? It's not even a ride. We didn't even get any food."

"Yes."

"Noki, did you do all this. All the fighting. All the training. Everything. Just to come to Walt Disney World?" joked Bug.

Noki just smiled and shrugged his shoulders.

Bug sat back as confused as ever. The silence continued. Then he started to look at the pictures on the wall. The area where they were sitting had murals from the movie Pinocchio. The little fast food snack restaurant was indeed called Pinocchio Haus. As Bug scanned each picture, inspecting a different scene from the movie, his heart began to beat faster and faster. The story unfolding in front of his eyes was eerily similar to the story of their lives.

"Jip, how did Noki get his nickname?" Bug asked in a nervous manner.

"He basically named himself. He just kept saying Noki over and over again when he was a kid. I told you he used to watch the same movies repeatedly but always pronounced the title wrong of this one picture. He shortened it", Jip said and startled to chuckle, "Hell, he wore that particular tape out. I must have replaced that same film three times".

"What was the name of the film?" Bug asked.

"Pinocchio".

CONCLUSION

All fables have some truth to them. All of them have a moral. This one is no different. Sometimes you save those in need and sometimes those same people save you. And that's okay. You just have to let them.

Gideon was suspended for a year and his purse for the big fight was given to a charity of Noki's choosing; the Special Olympics. John was also suspended but for life. Stan Kotch lost his promoter's license and all of his wealth because he bet everything against Noki. This bet was placed illegally because promotors can't be seen as biased. The problem was he made this massive bet with Pepe Grillo. And no one ever saw Stan again. "He wrote a check his ass couldn't cash", Limpy said.

The crew lived happily ever after. Bug paid his debt, now to Frank, and had a clean slate in life. Jip retired from running the gym and gave that responsibility to Bug. Carlo's Gym was finally renamed Noki's Gym and the place went through a much needed renovation to make it more upscale and hospitable for the boxers, especially the white-collar professionals who were pouring in there to train. Limpy's plan was a magnificent success. Fay got her job back but always kept in touch with the team and even went to the gym there to learn some boxing and to work out herself. She lost a bunch of weight, too, and she always wore her trademark blue colors. Bug tried to get Frank Calzone to come and do the same, but he just laughed.

Noki helped out by teaching all the real boxers to use different styles that would help them in their upcoming fights. He still would train at 10:02 PM and Bug was always there to watch. Bug finally asked him why he would train at the same time and Noki's response was, "Papa always says to tend to business". And Bug realized that Noki still took some things literally. Just another quirk for the real boy named Tyrone Polendina.

And Noki planned on never fighting again.

ACKNOWLEDGEMENTS

This book is an homage to many of my favorite experiences in life. I hope no one is offended by it because that is not the intent. I love boxing, and all the great champions, but there is still so much wrong with the sport. The underbelly and characters involved are exposed only a little here. The sport can be so much better and safer. The reality is that no one cares about these fighters, especially after they are done. Many, if not most, start from poverty and end back up there when they are done. The only difference is the brain damage they incur. Again, there is no help given to them. I did want to point out some of the greatest boxers the world has ever seen and to show their different styles and techniques. It is not just a street fight. It is an art.

I have always had a special spot in my heart for the disabled, the odd people, the quirky people and so on. They are marginalized and have more gifts than any of us will ever know. We just don't give them a chance. Autism is still an enigma to us. As a doctor, they have been some of my favorite patients to treat over the past thirty years. They always make my day when they came in and they always make me smile. I thank them for that. I do not know of any autistic person being a savant in sports like Noki. There have been endless cases of autistic savants in music and art, however. I even had an autistic child patient who would watch a movie and then write all the credits perfectly after watching them. His room was filled with pages of them and they were perfectly correct, and this was before he was old enough for school!

Lastly, if this tale reminds you of any fable or Disney movie then you would be correct. I apologize if anyone thought I took liberties in using this as a framework for this story, but that movie was my favorite of all time and it was just a need for me to express this love via a book. And if anyone asks, the answer would be yes, I wrote the character of Bug with Peter Dinklage in mind. He is one of my favorite actors of all time.

Glossary of Real Fighters Highlighted in Noki

1. Muhammad Ali

2. Alexia Arguello

3. Joe Frazier

4. Bill Conn

5. Jack Dempsey

6. Floyd Mayweather Jr.

7. Willie Pep

8. Bruce "The Mouse" Strauss

9. Pernell Whitaker

10. Benny Leonard

11. James Toney

12. Roberto Duran

13. Marco Antonio Barrera

14. Winky Wright

15. Roy Jones, Jr.

16. Joe Louis

17. Julio Caeser Chavez Sr.

18. Oscar De La Hoya

19. Juan Manuel Marquez

20. Freddie Pendleton

21. Archie Moore

22. Orlando Canizales

23. James J. Braddock

24. Sugar Ray Leonard

25. Marvin Hagler

DO NOT LOOK AT THE NEXT PAGE
UNTIL YOU HAVE READ THE BOOK

Easter Eggs and Pinocchio references:

1. This really is the story of Pinocchio told in a different way. When Bug realizes that the murals look like their life story, he is correct.

2. Carlo's Gym – Carlo Collodi wrote Pinocchio.

3. Bug (Jim Grillo) – Jiminy Cricket. Bug also comes out of nowhere out of the rain like Jiminy did in the movie. Jim stands for Jiminy. Grillo is Italian for cricket.

4. Jip – short for Giuseppe Polendina - Geppetto is a variant of Giuseppe

5. Noki Tyrone Polendina – He is Pinocchio, many mentions of how he wants to be a real boy, how he is lifeless and wooden due to his autistic quirks. It is also how he would pronounce Pinocchio as a kid and he nicknamed himself Noki.

6. Polendina – means a yellow wig and it is what Geppetto wore in the original Collodi book.

7. Limpy – Lampwick or Lampy as Pinocchio would call his friend in the animated movie.

8. John – Honest John, the fox and evil character in the animated movie.

9. Lionel Gideon – Gideon, the cat who is with Honest John in the animated movie.

10. Fay – Blue Fairy, Fay is a term used for Fairy, she wears a blue outfit, Godmother is mentioned.

11. Monstro the whale – it is the rehab/nursing home system that Fay did not want Jip to be swallowed by.

12. Shining star – Jip and Bug all wish upon a star.

13. Frank Calzone – Stromboli, a puppeteer in both movies, the food calzone is not the same thing as Stromboli but they are similar.

14. Stan Kotch – Coachman (the evil character who gathers the boys in the animated movie to turn them into donkeys), Kotch is how Kocs is pronounced, which stands for a Hungarian town where the term "coachman" came from.

15. Las Vegas – Pleasure Island from the movie, this was how Kotch tried to impress Noki and team with the penthouse, Cirque De Soleil and toys.

16. Shadowy figures mentioned by Kotch - Shadowy figures who gather the boys at pleasure island in the original animated film.

17. Pepe Grillo – "pepper cricket", originally from Collodi story and was the name for Jiminy Cricket.

18. "Like a bolt out of the blue Fate steps in and sees you through" – Jip says this, song from When You Wish Upon A Star.

19. When You Wish Upon A Star – Entrance music used by Noki.

20. Dr. Roy Walt – stands for Roy and Walt Disney.

21. Vest worn by Jip and his antique musket – what Geppetto wears and has in the animated movie.

22. Goldfish and cat - Cleo and Figaro.

23. Jip like to make clocks, snored a lot and both were loud – all from original movie.

24. Quotes: Stan Kotch "I always say, give a bad boy enough rope and he'll soon make a jackass of himself", Bug: "And then they never come back as boys, do they? ". Both are said by Coachman in animated movie.

ABOUT THE AUTHOR

Douglas Farrago MD is a retired family doctor. He is the author of multiple books on what is called Direct Primary Care. He also the author of two humorous books: *The Placebo Chronicles* and *Diary of a Drug Rep*. Dr. Farrago is also the inventor of a product called the Knee Saver for baseball catchers and the Cryohelmet used by athletes for head injuries as well as migraine sufferers.

Prior to becoming a physician, Doug was an amateur boxer in college and thought about becoming a pro like his brother Matt. Fortunately, he wasn't good enough and decided to quit. After that he was hired by the Houston Boxing Association to help work with the fighters in nutrition and conditioning. He worked with many champions during this time. Much of his experiences in boxing during those years formed the stories in this book.

Made in the USA
Columbia, SC
31 March 2021